DOLPHIN COLORING BOOK

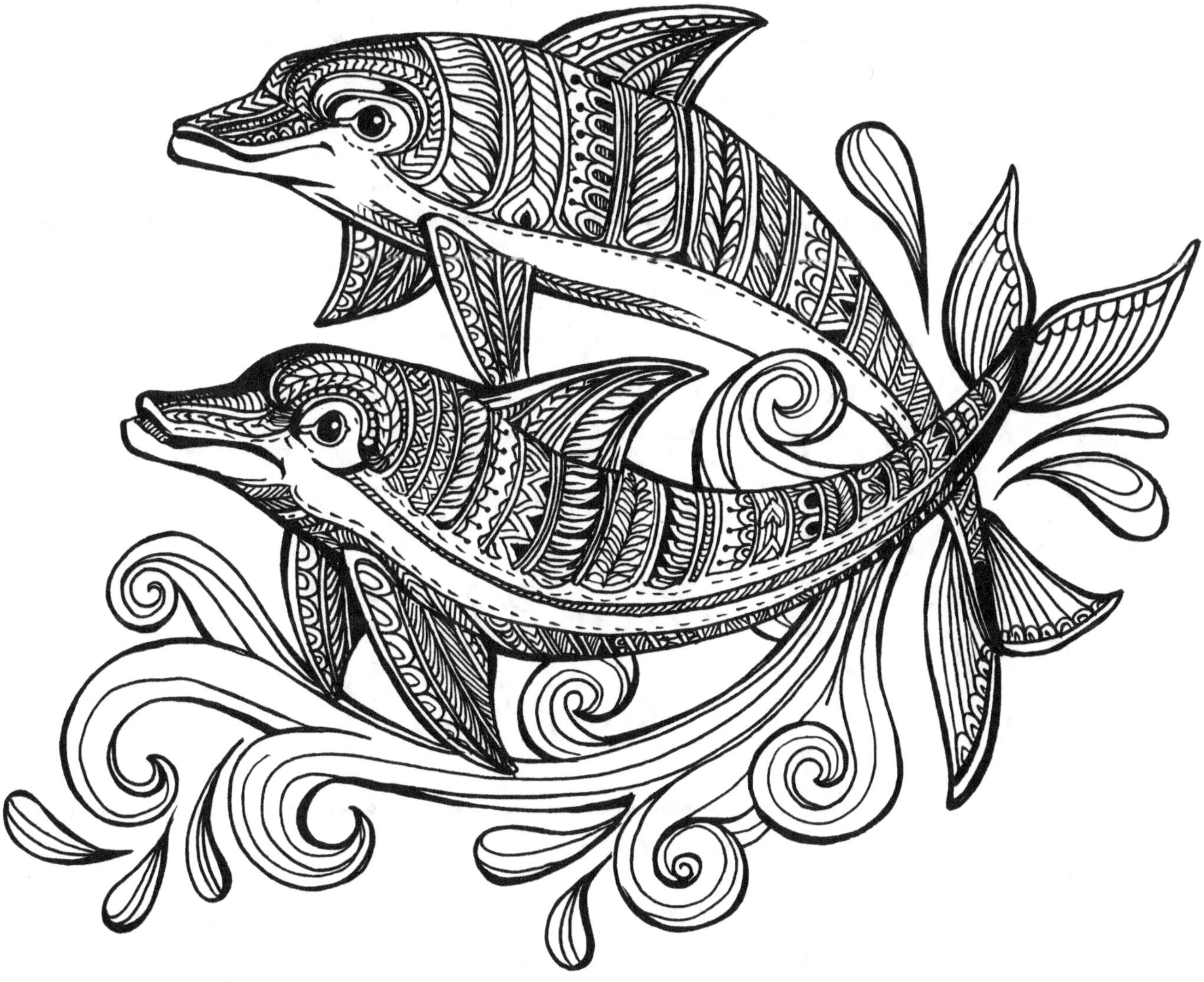

- RUSS FOCUS -

ISBN-13: 978-1727053906 ISBN-10: 1727053907

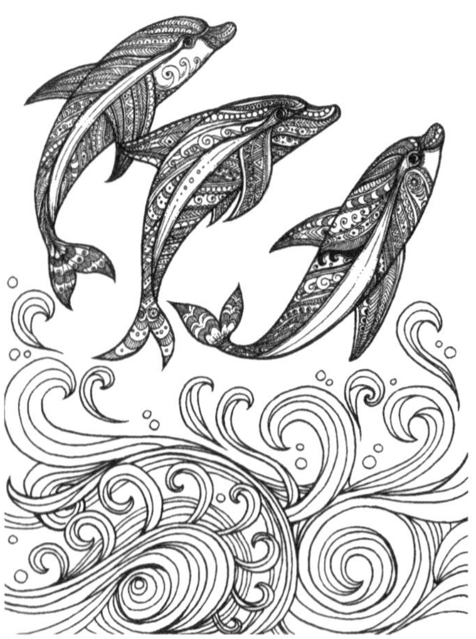

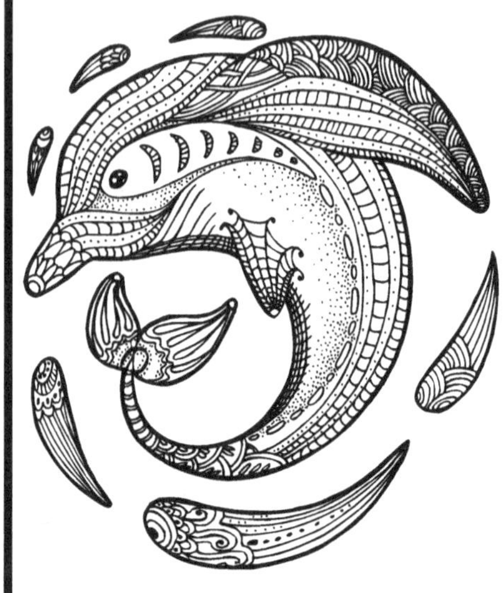

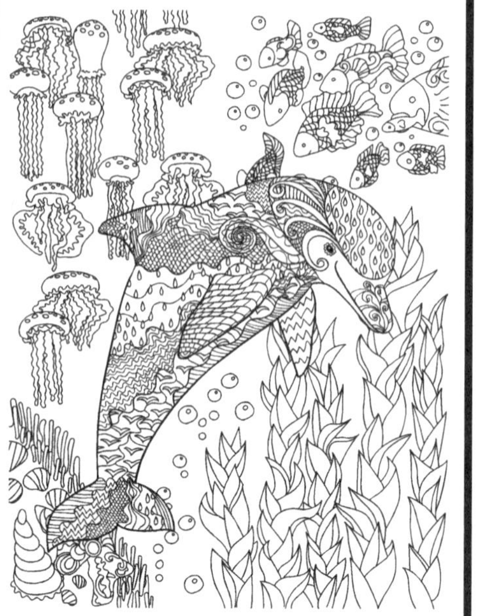

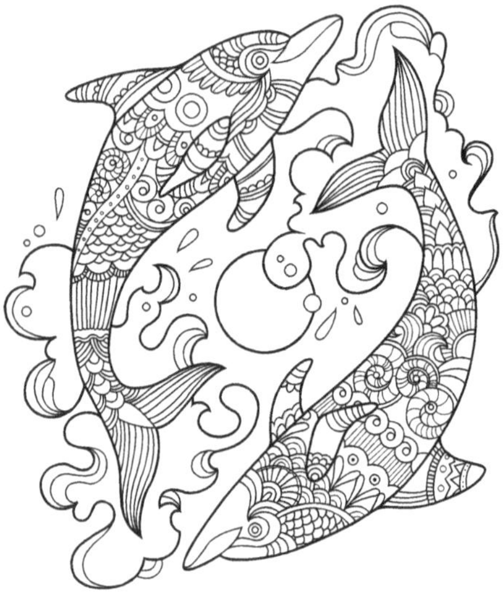

SAMPLE
DOLPHIN
COLORING
17 of 37
PAGES

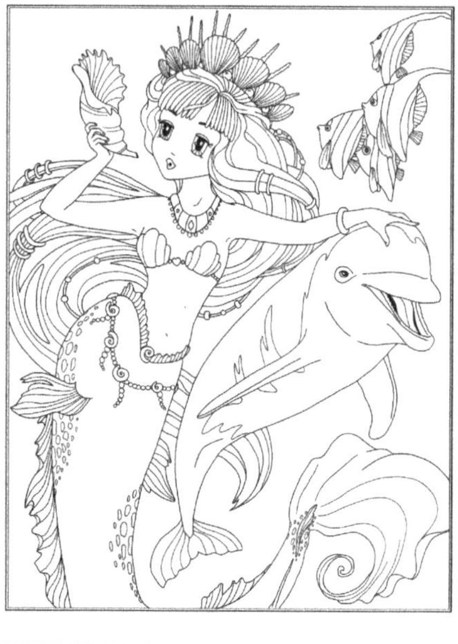

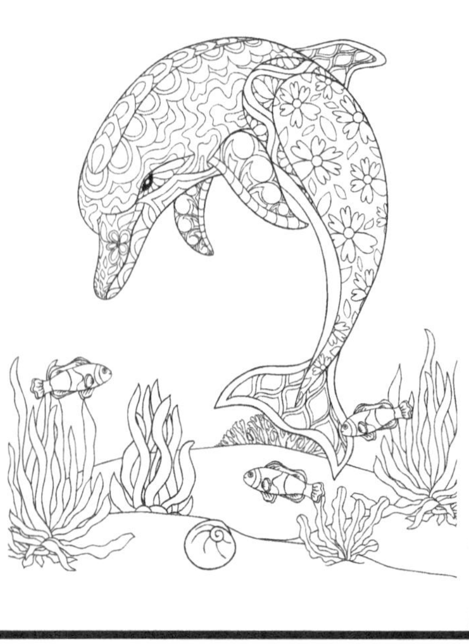

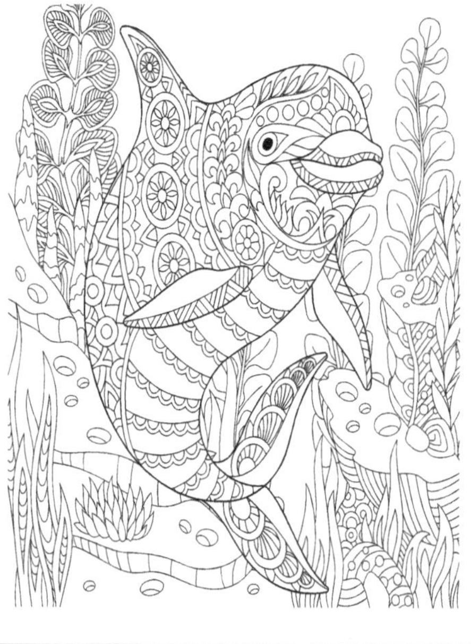

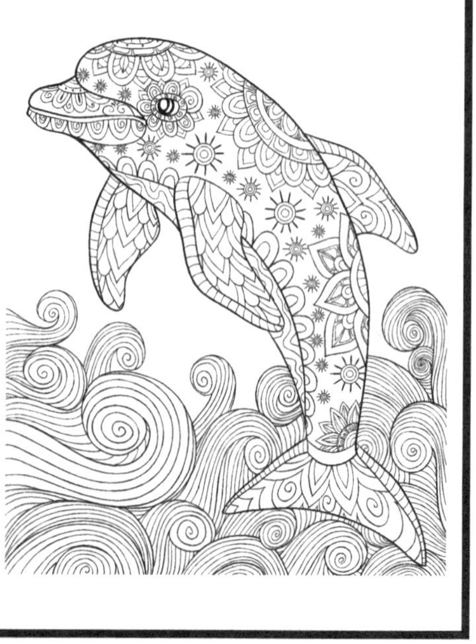

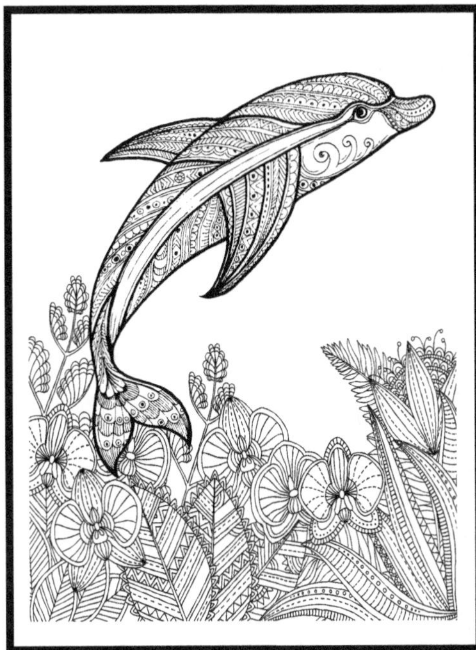
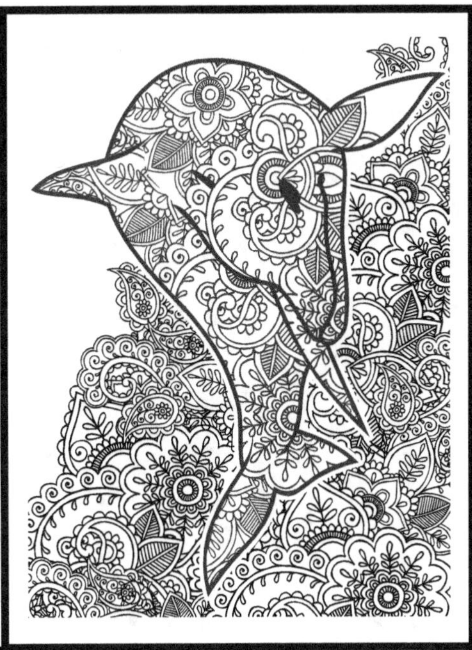
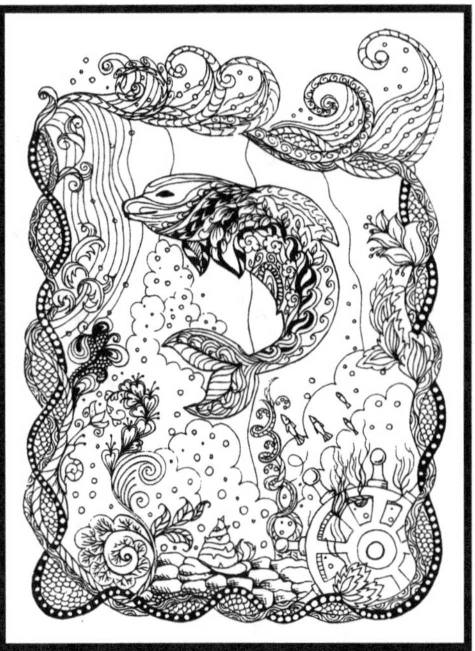
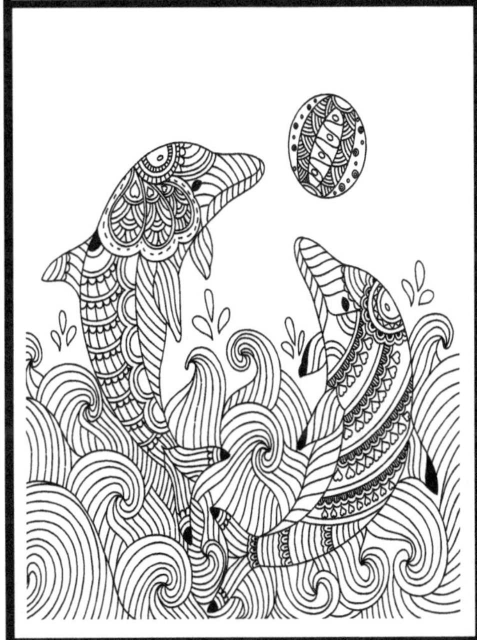
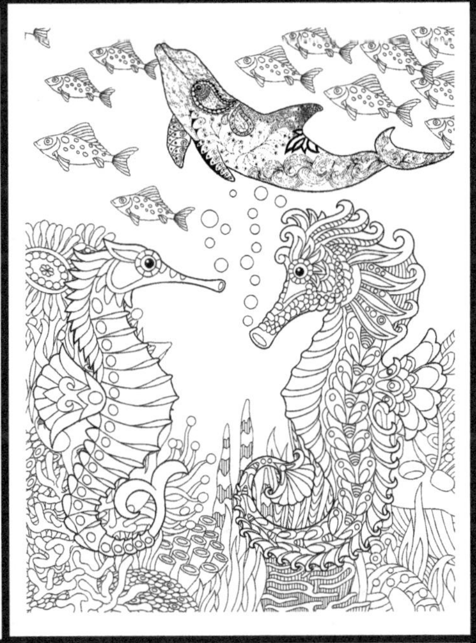
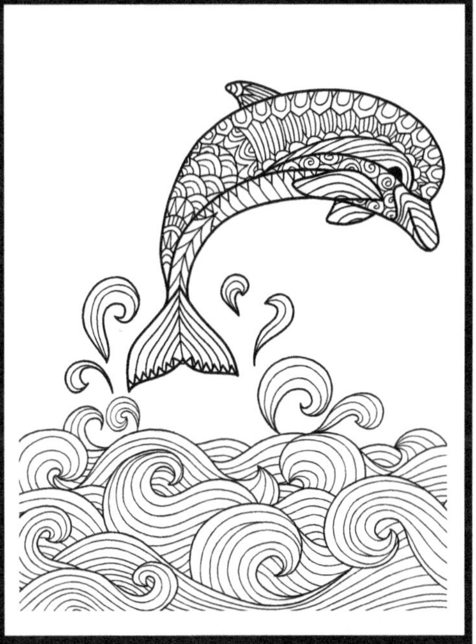
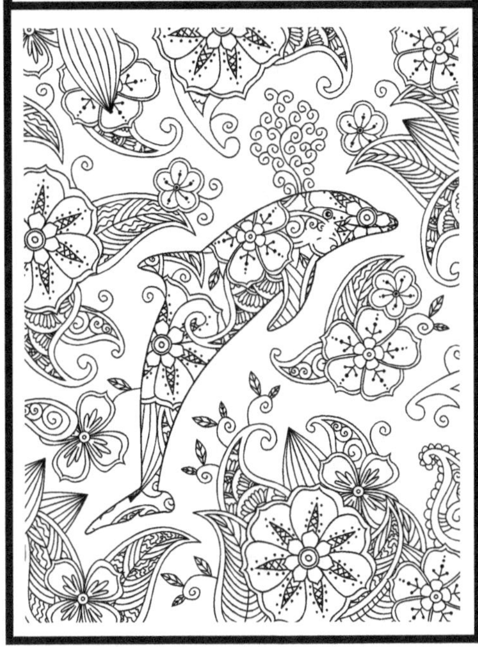
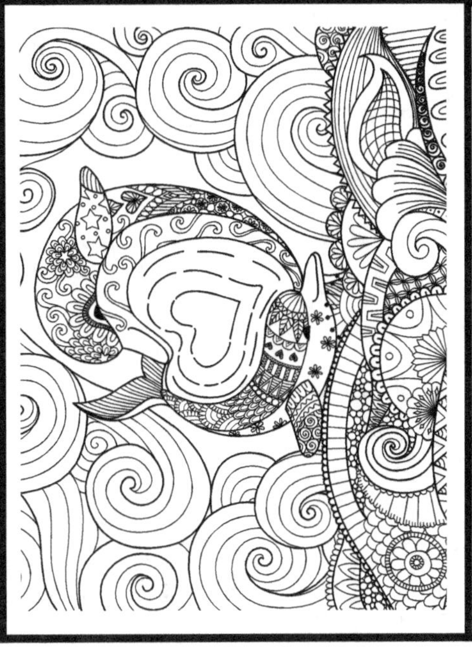
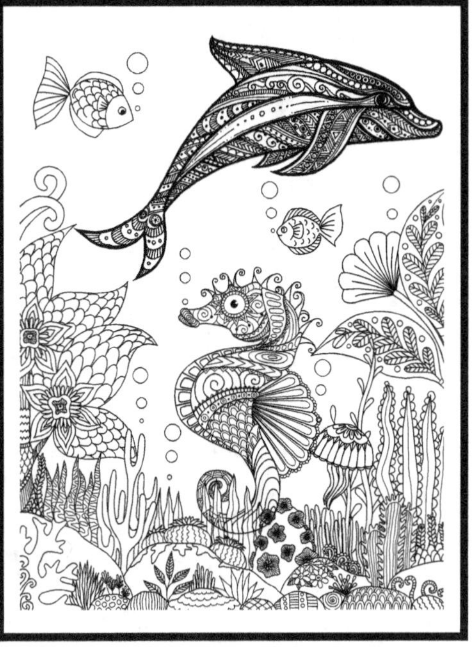

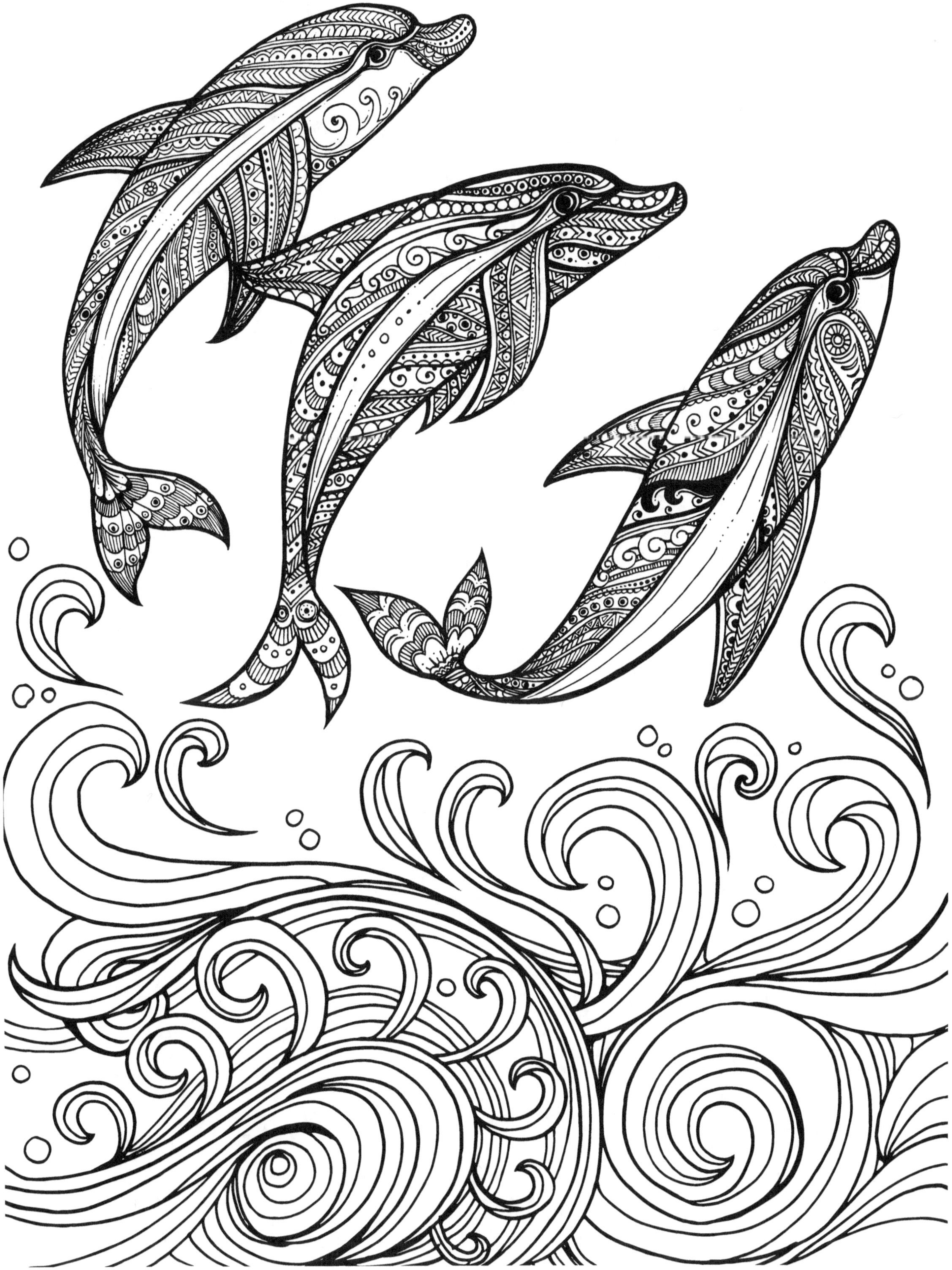

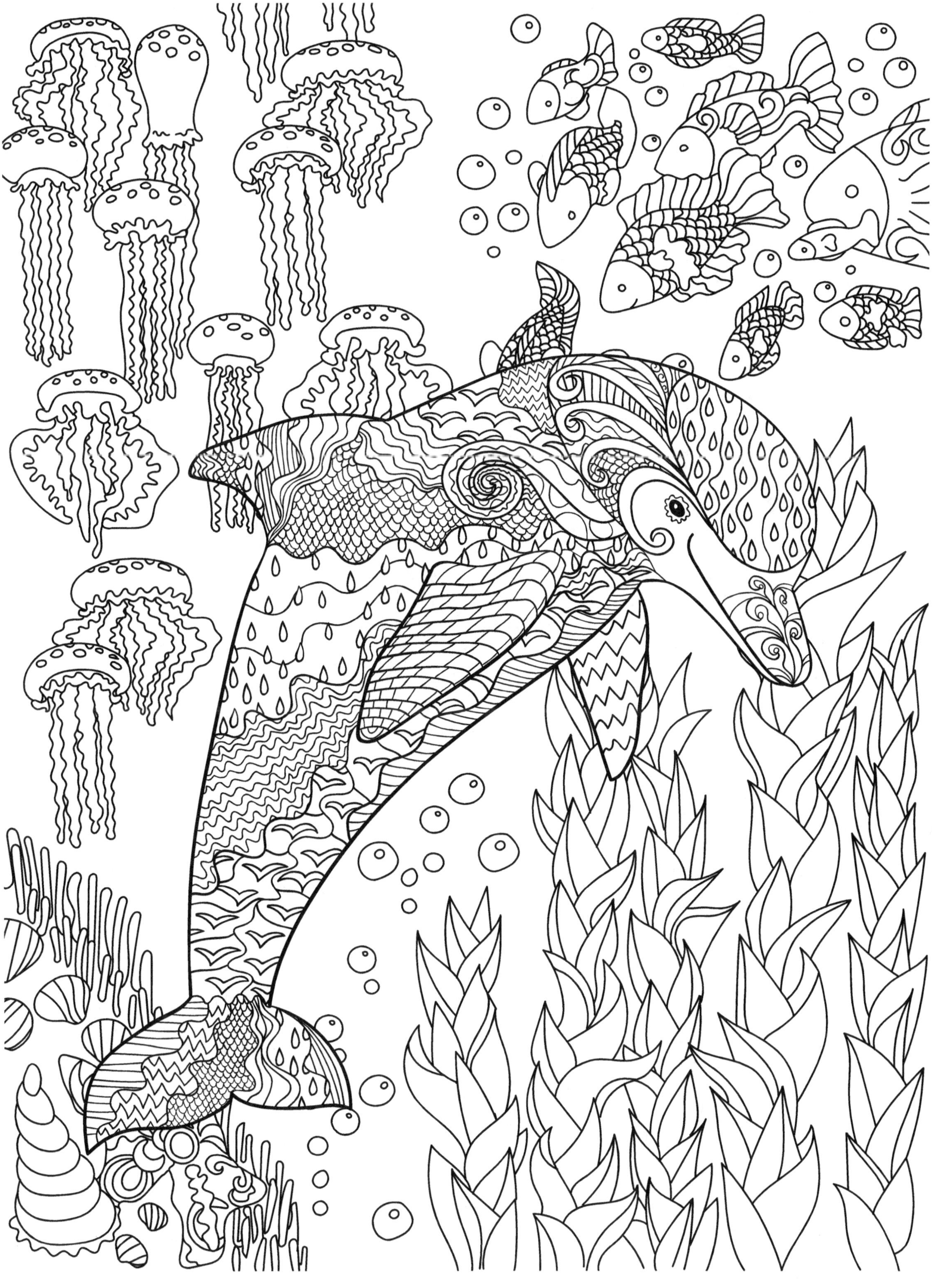

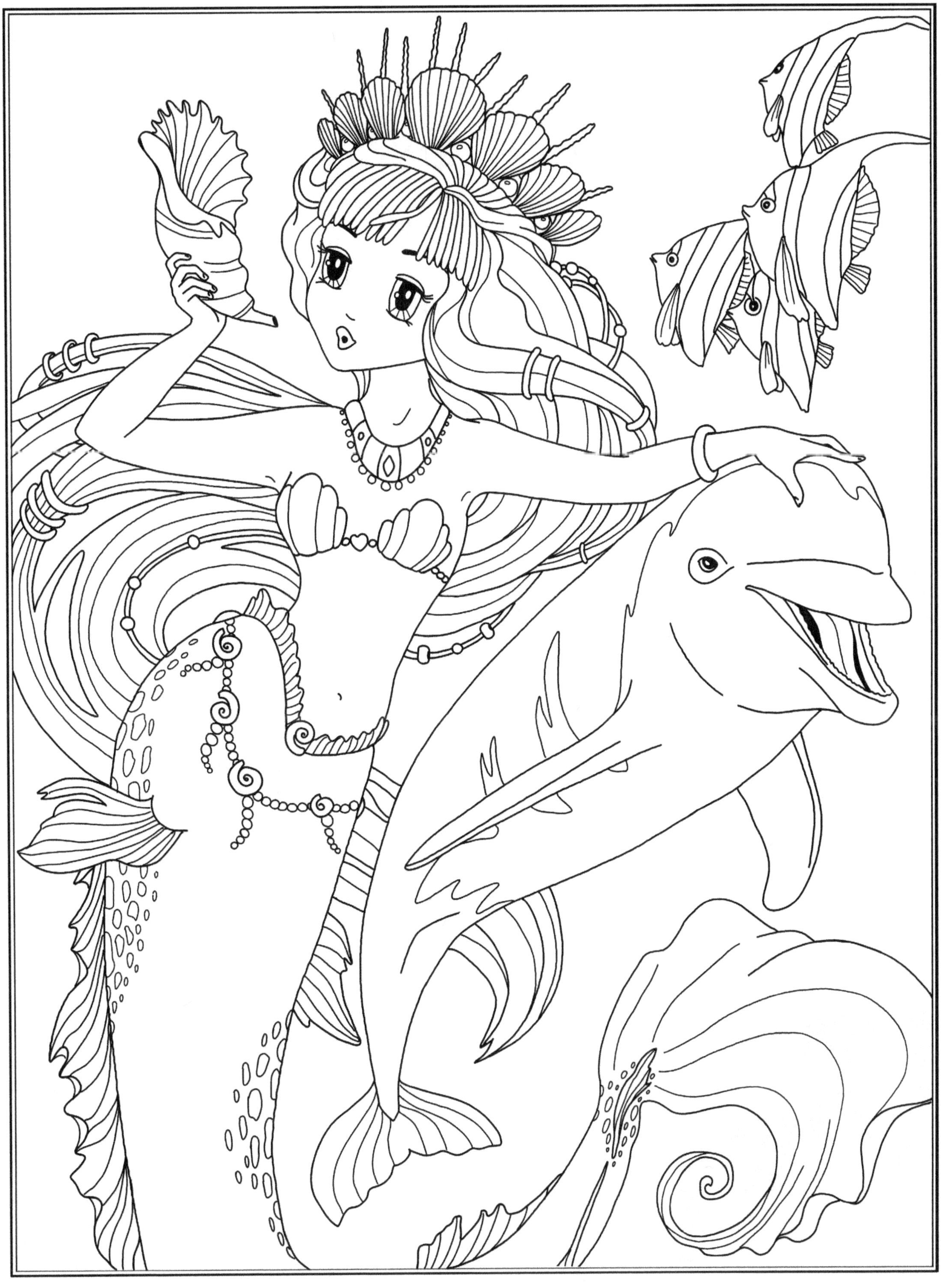

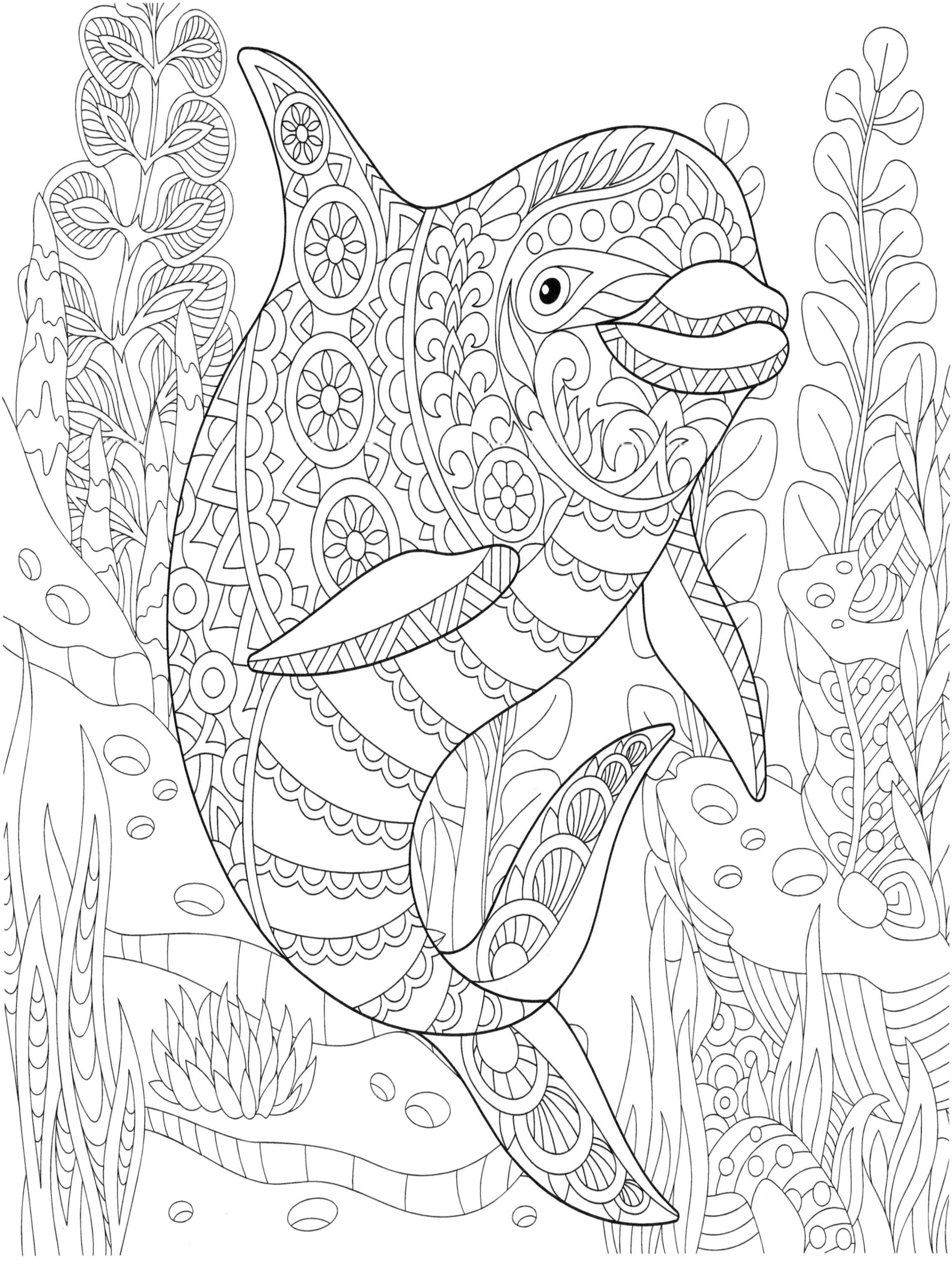

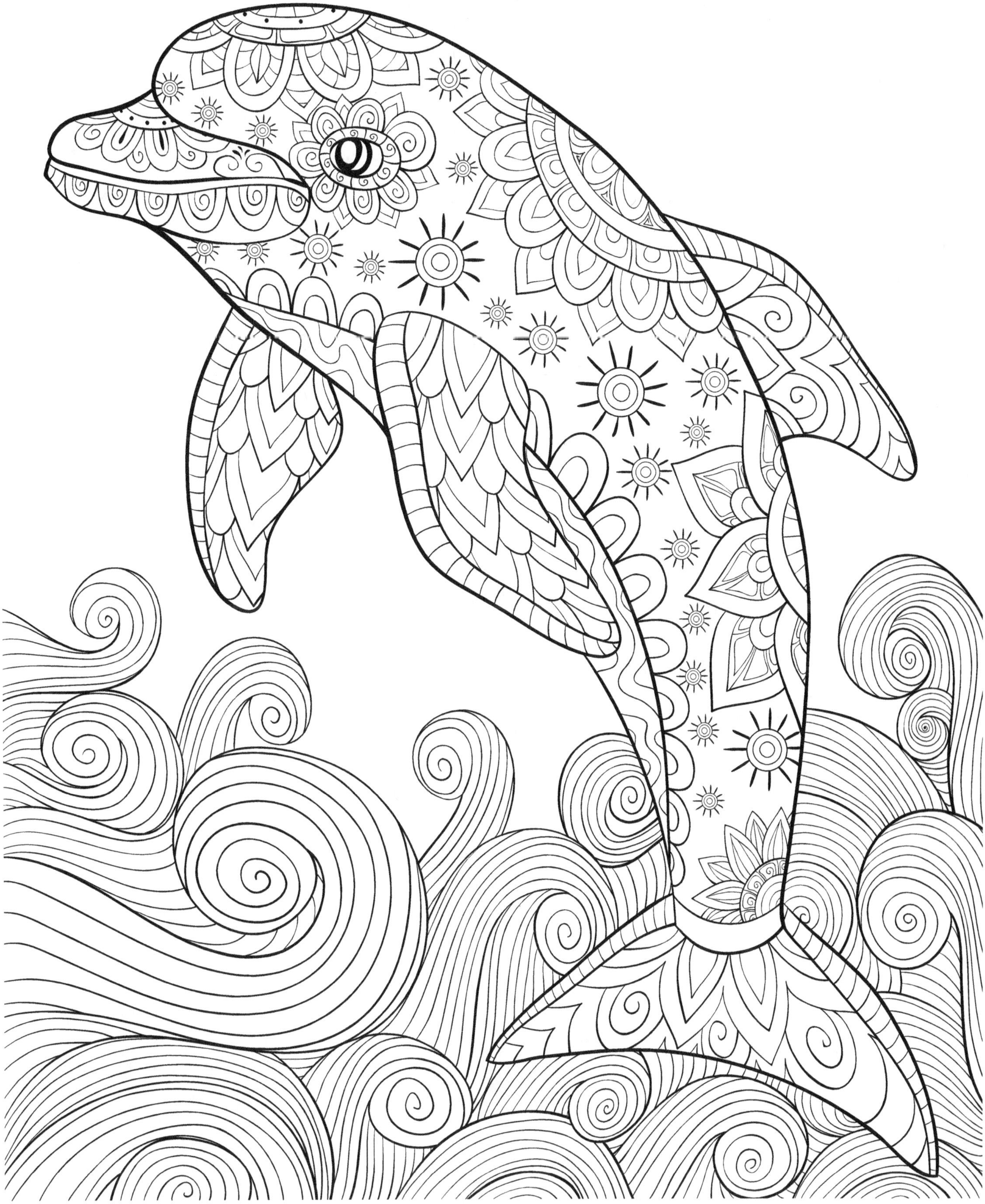

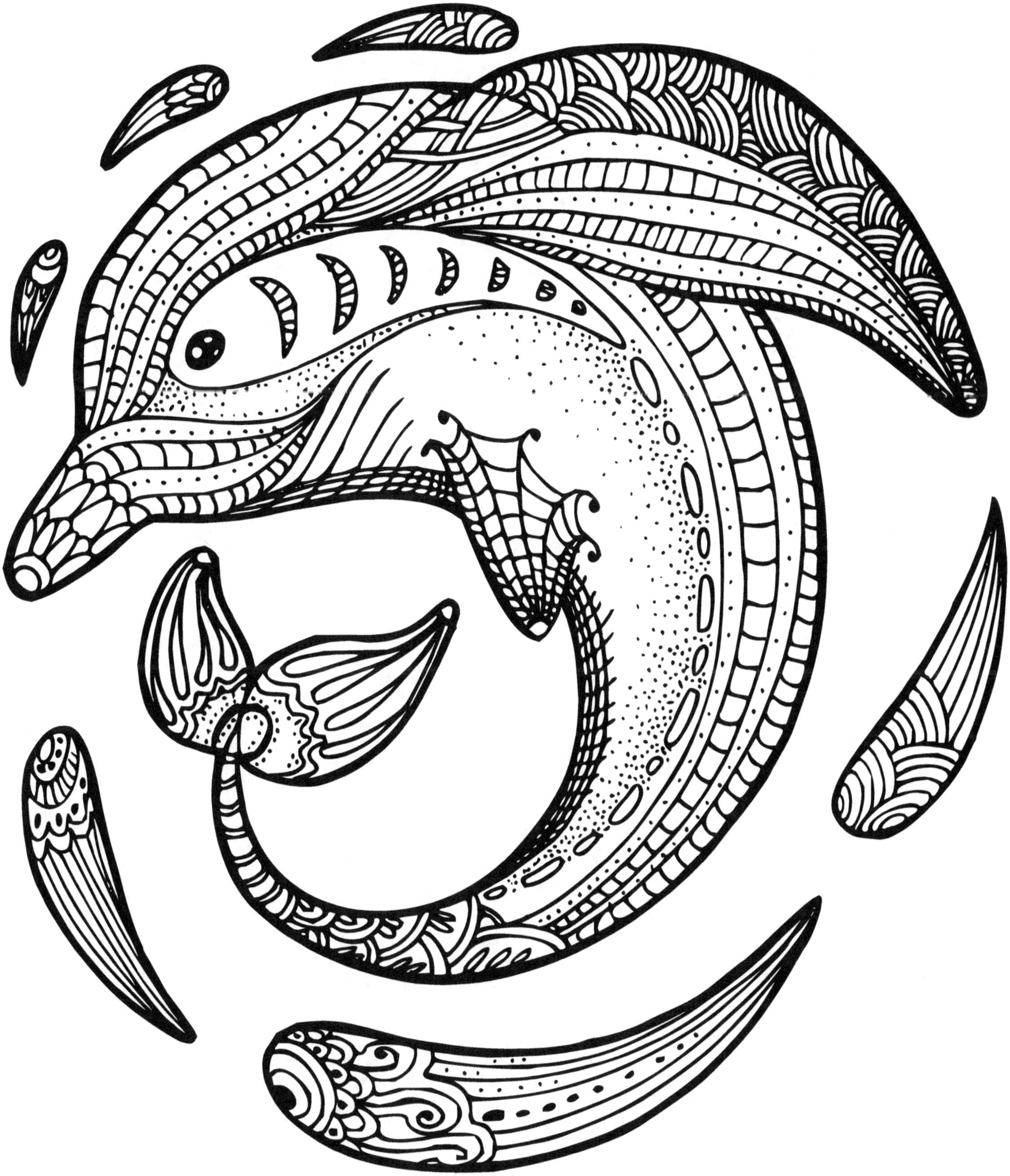

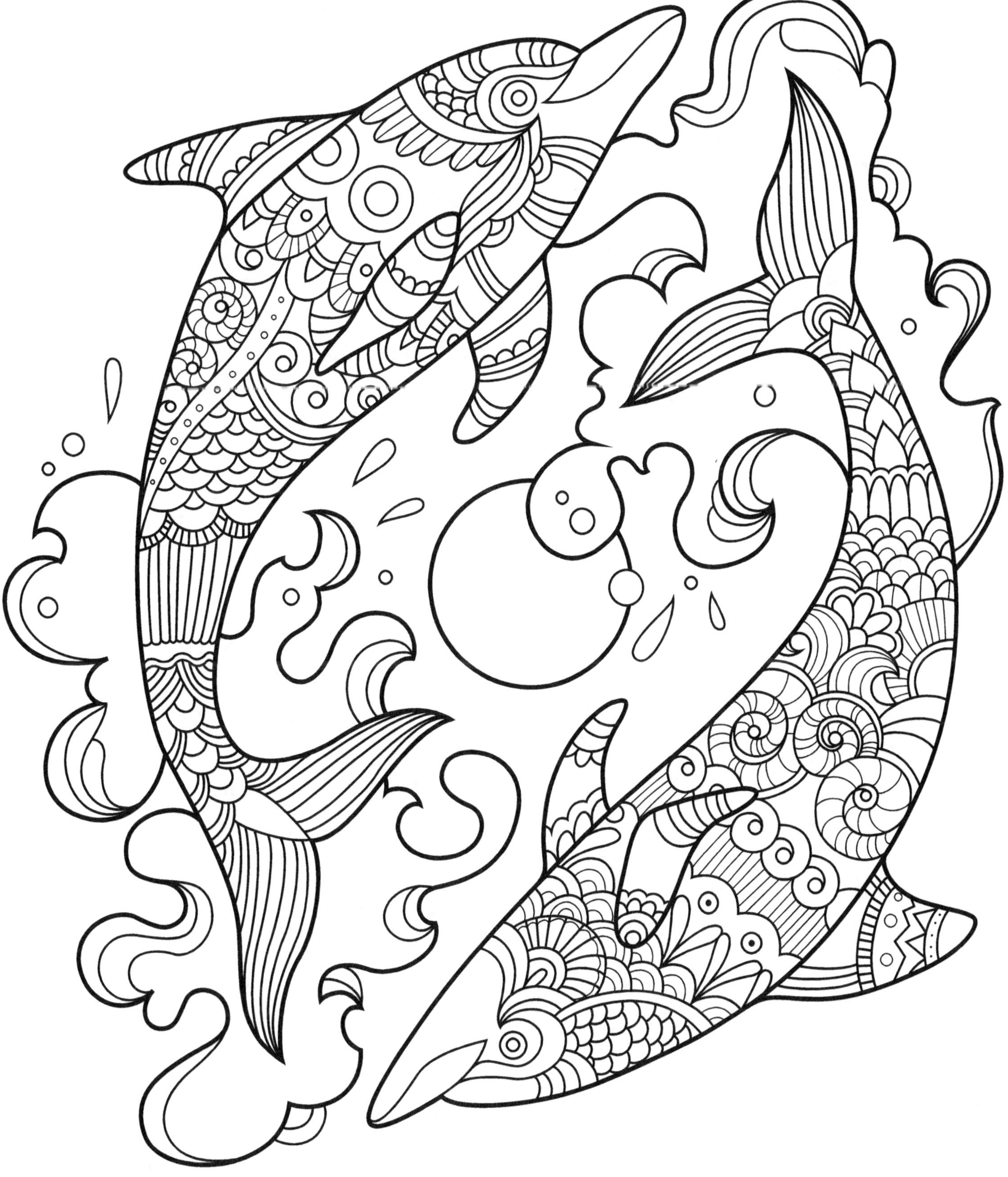

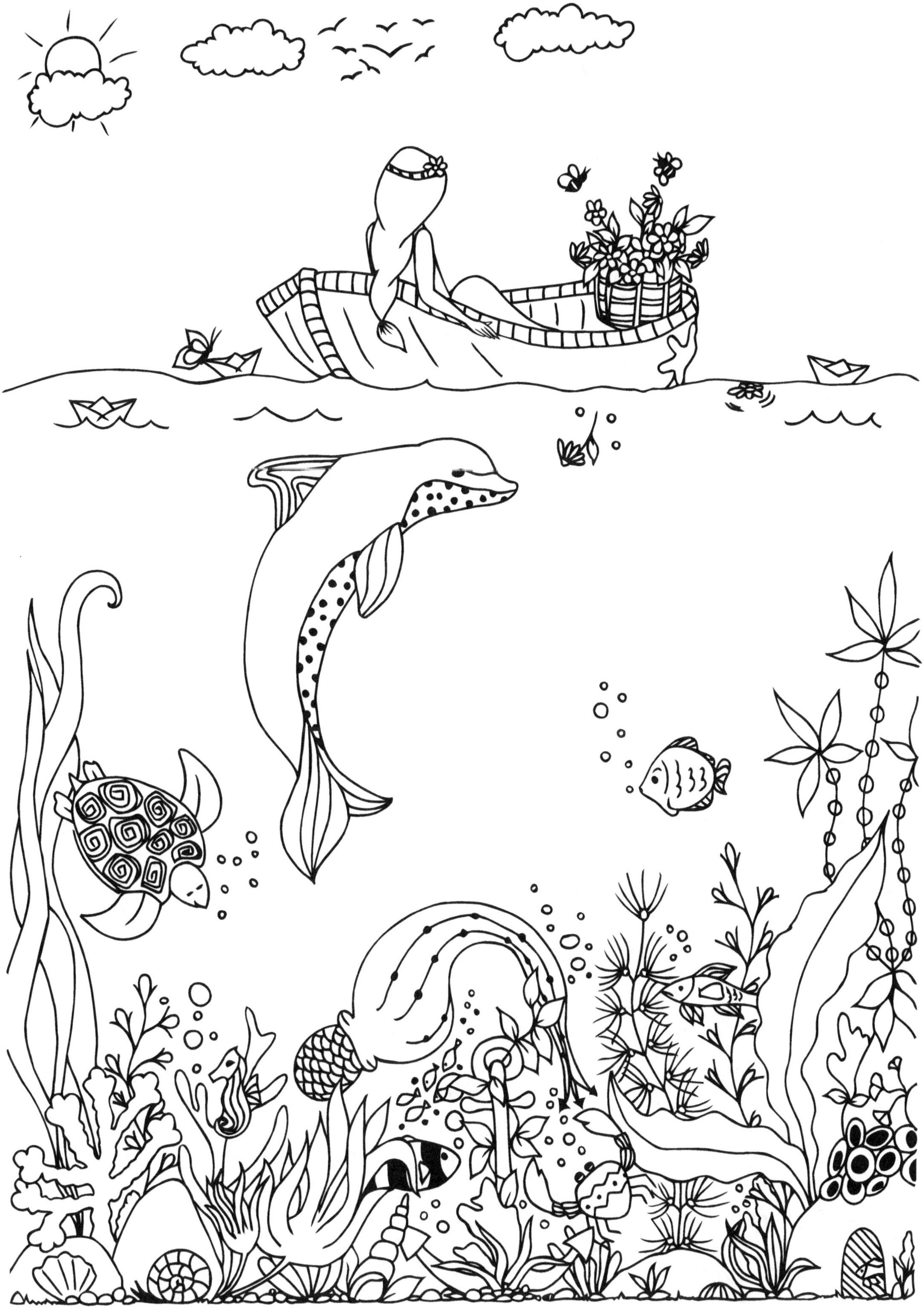

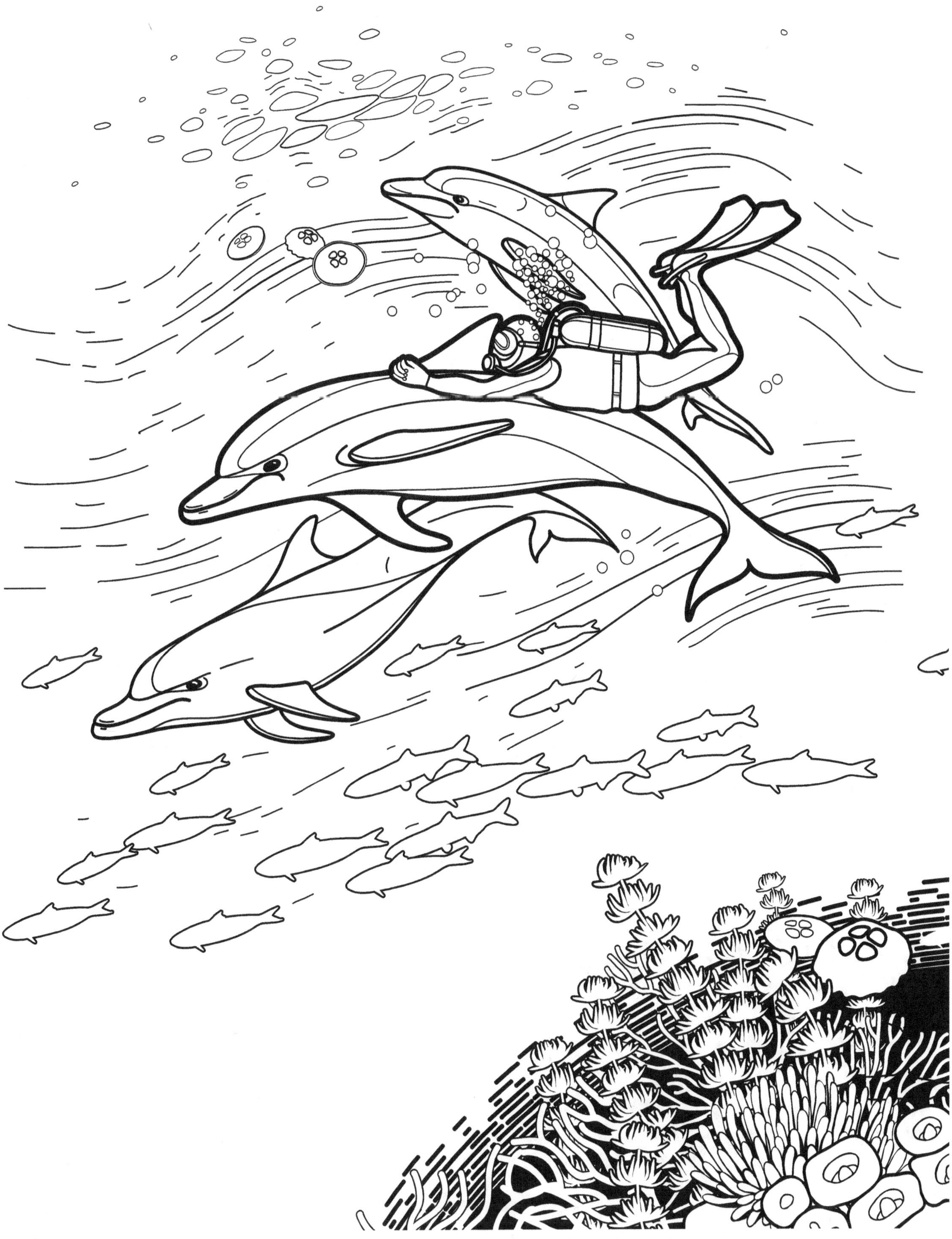

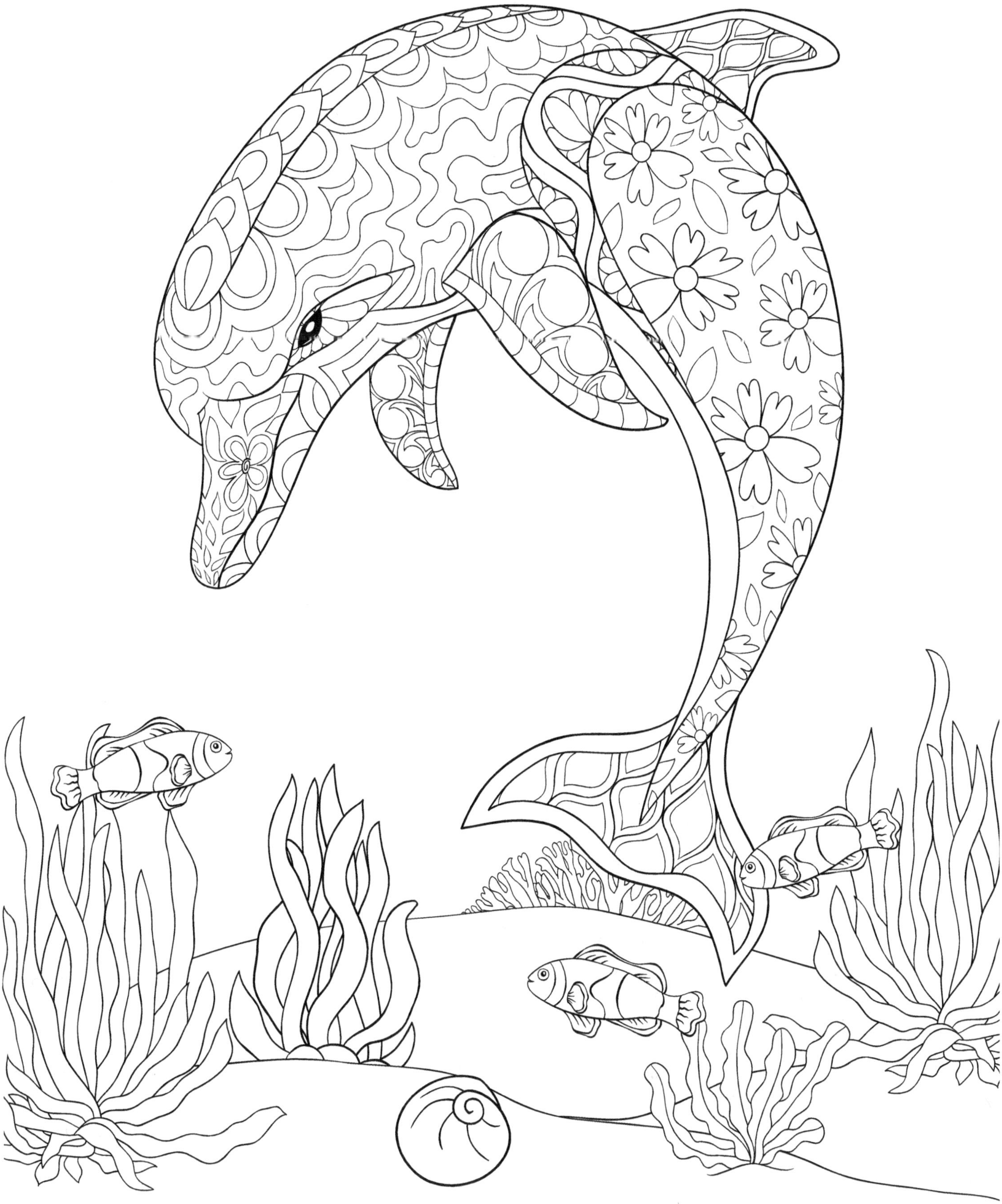

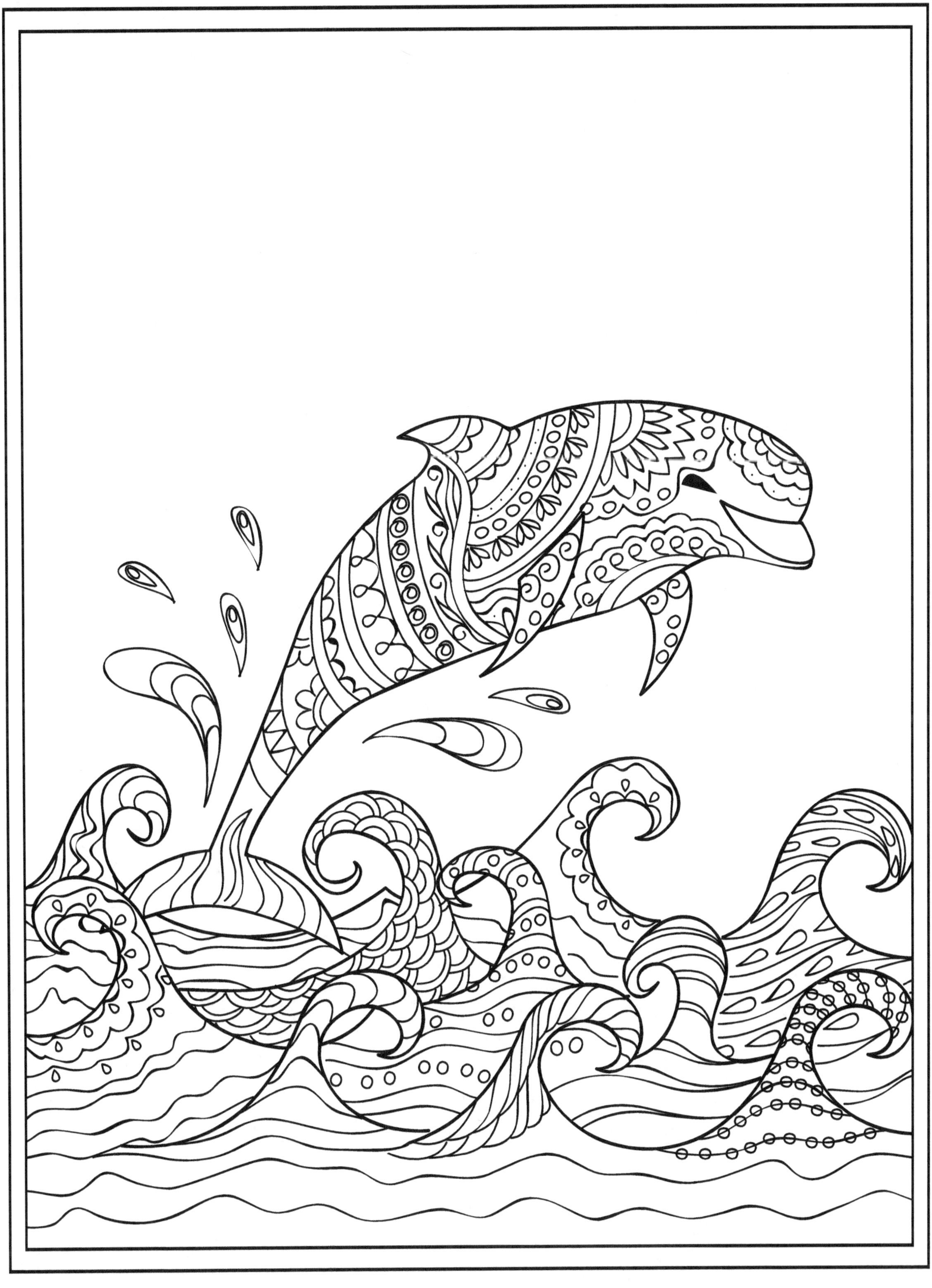

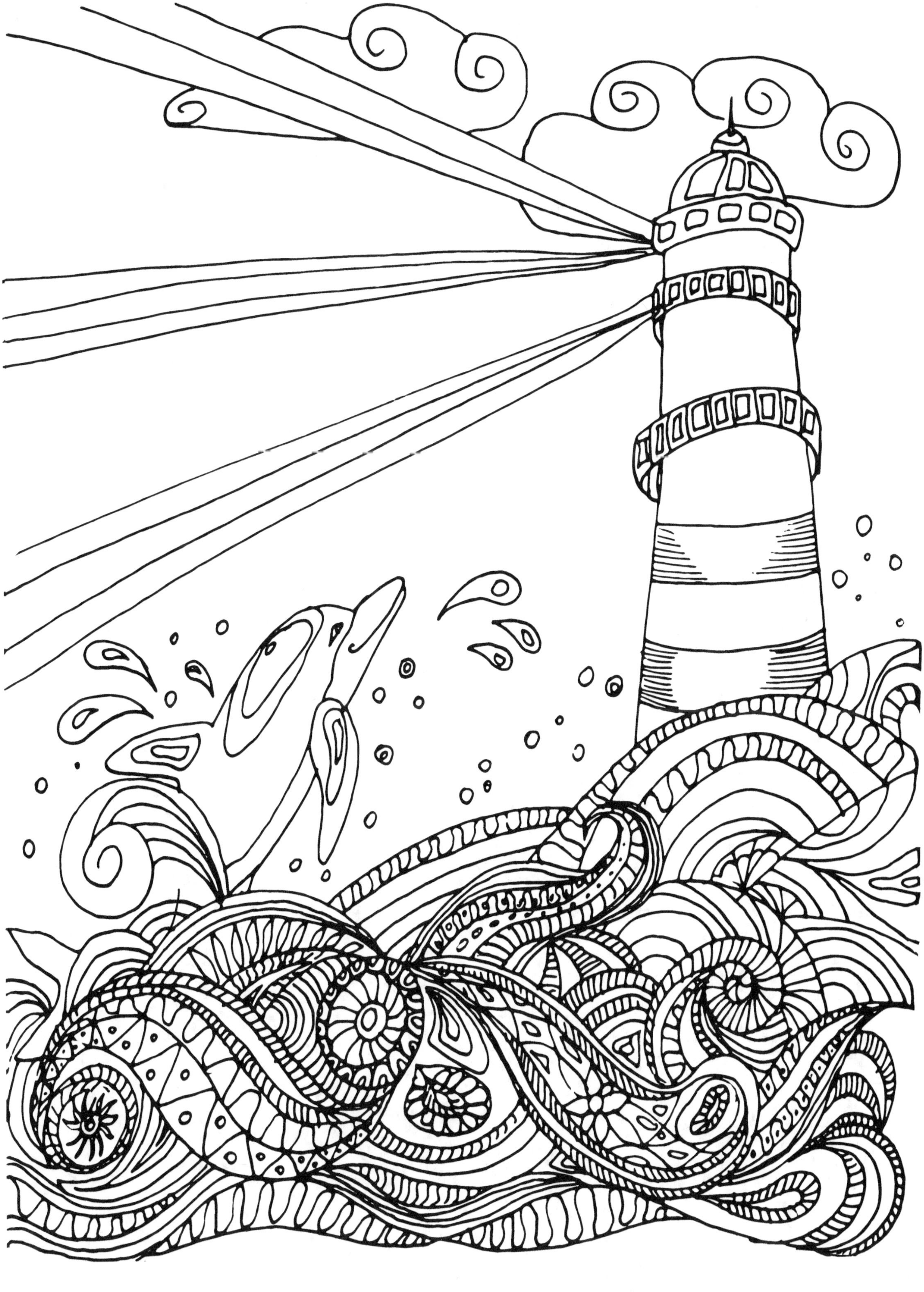

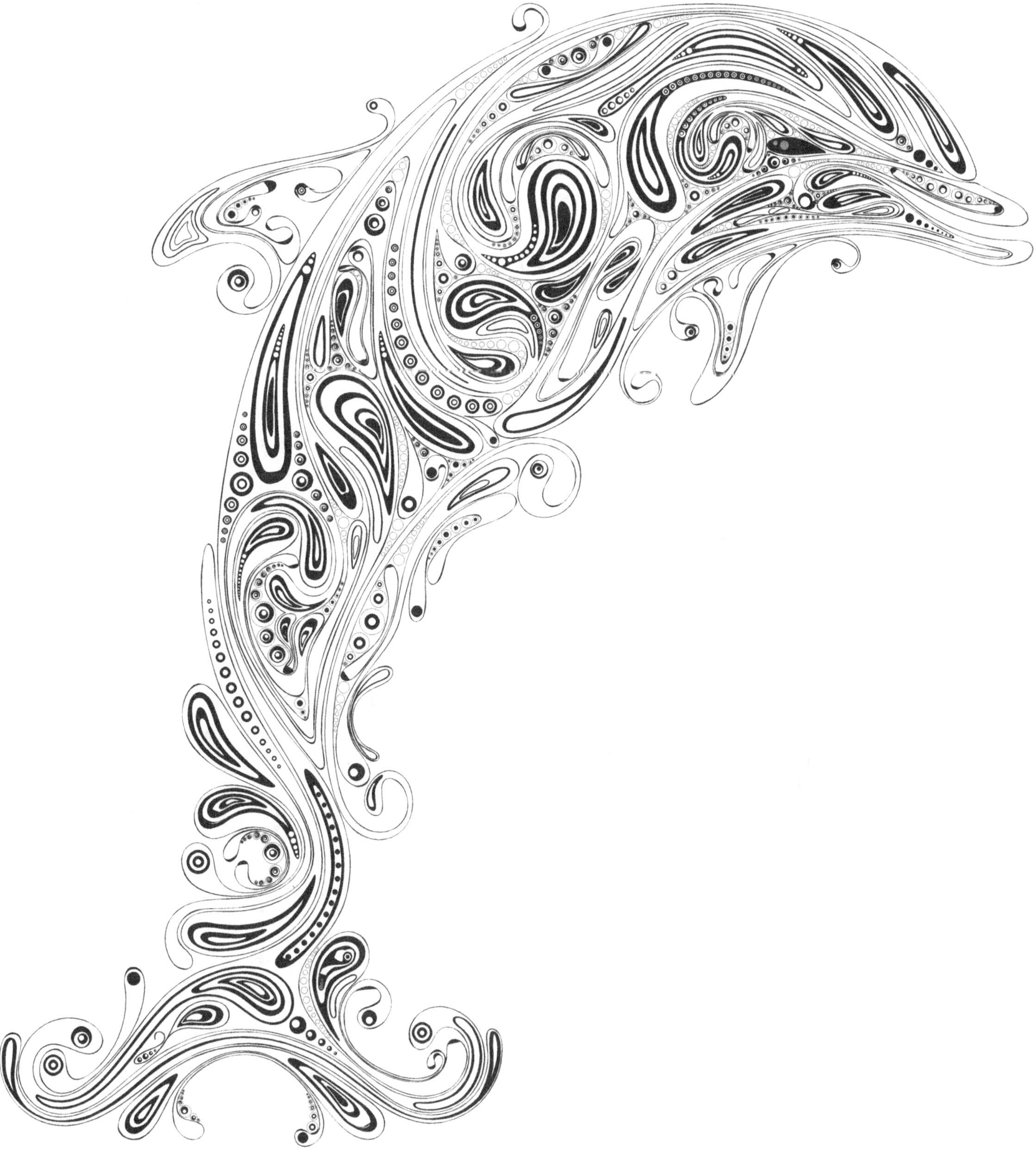

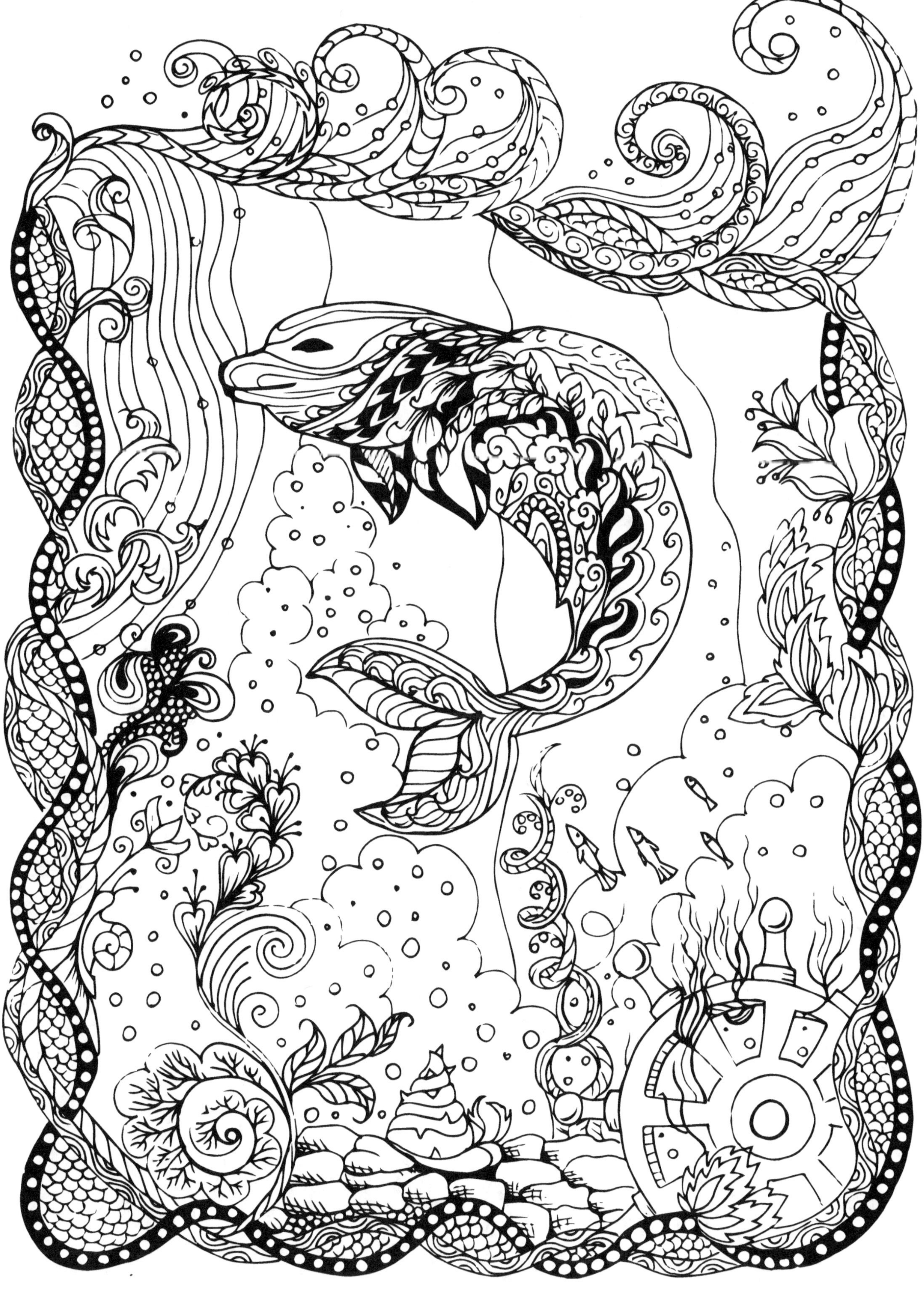

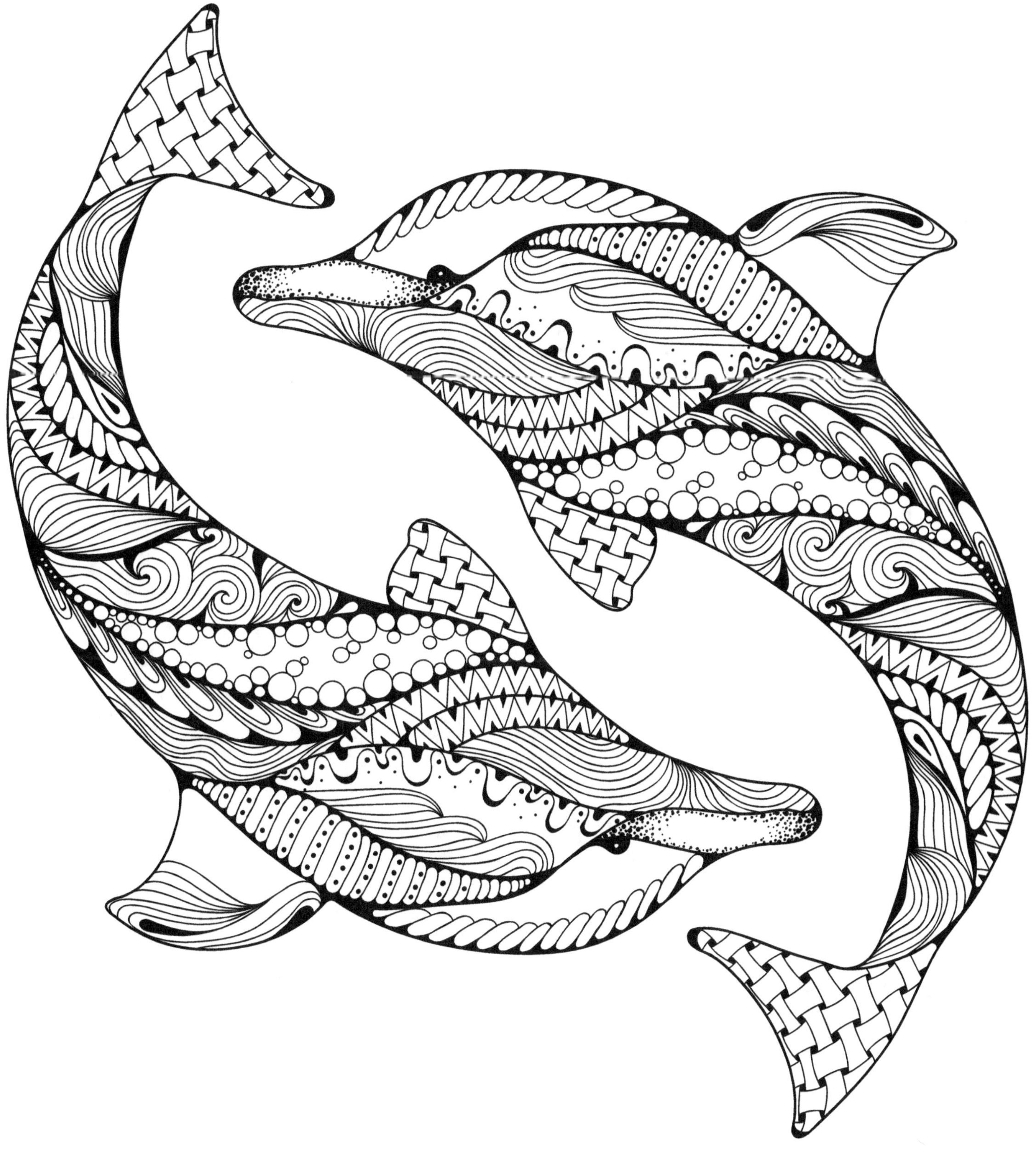

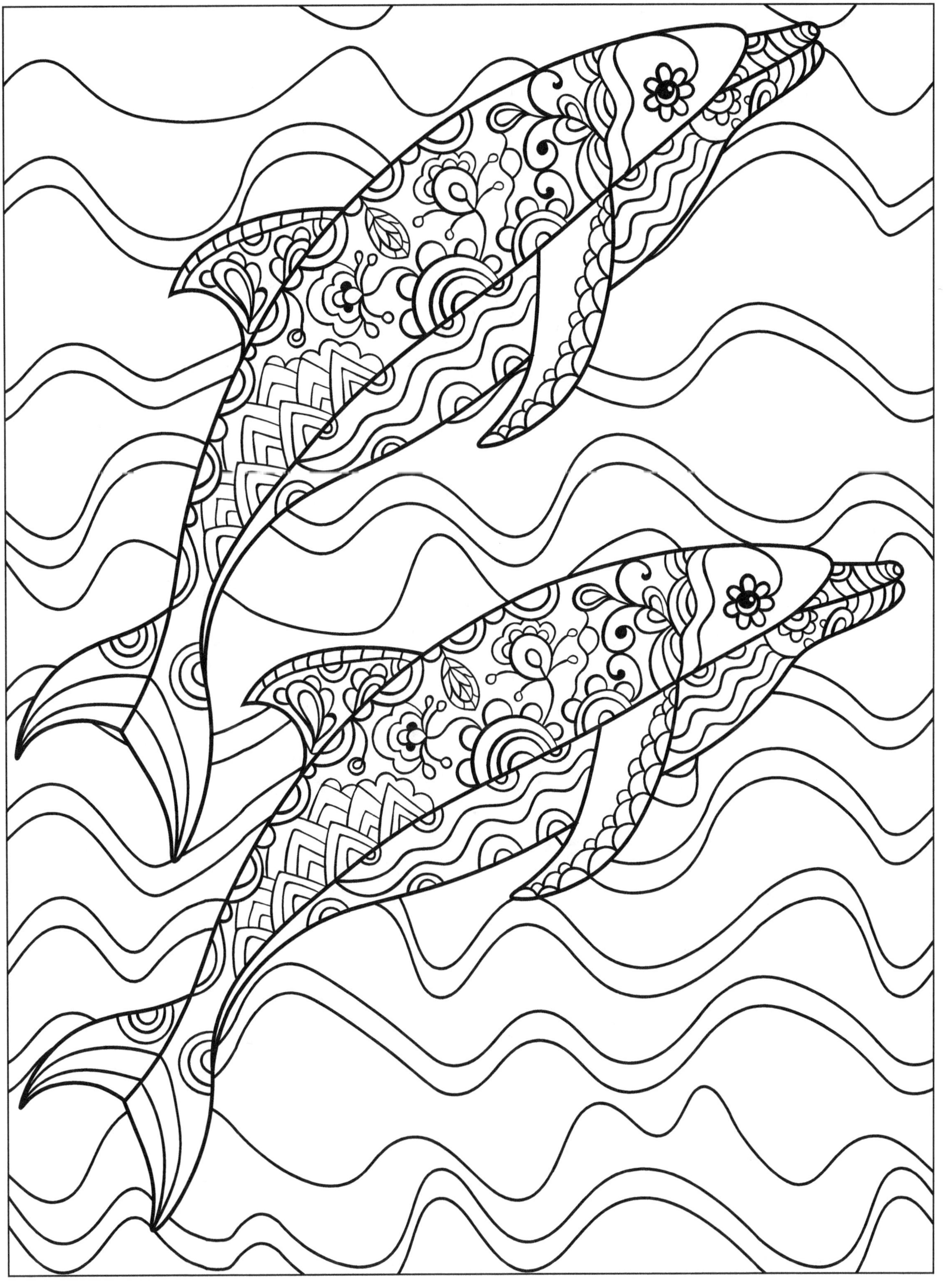

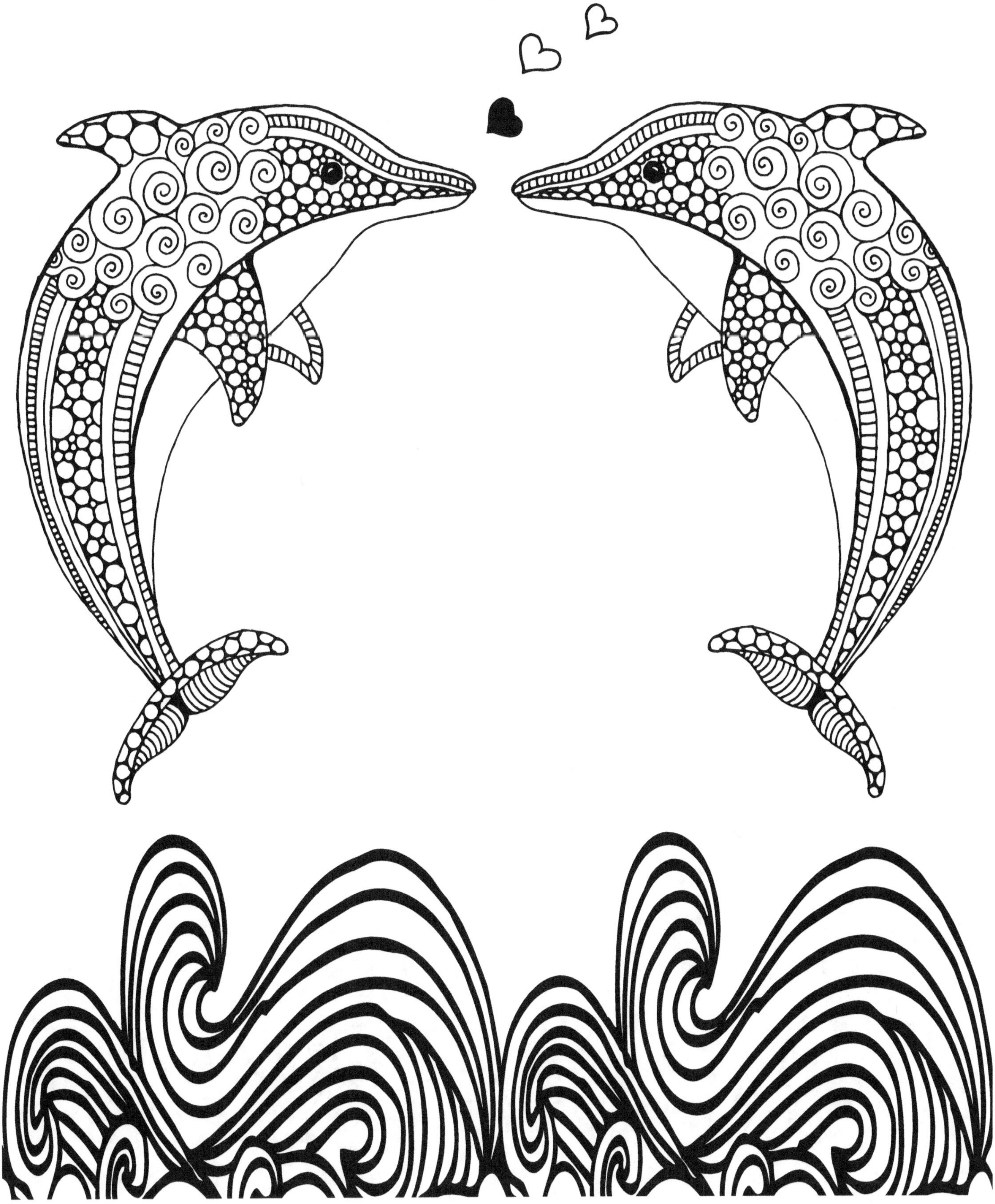

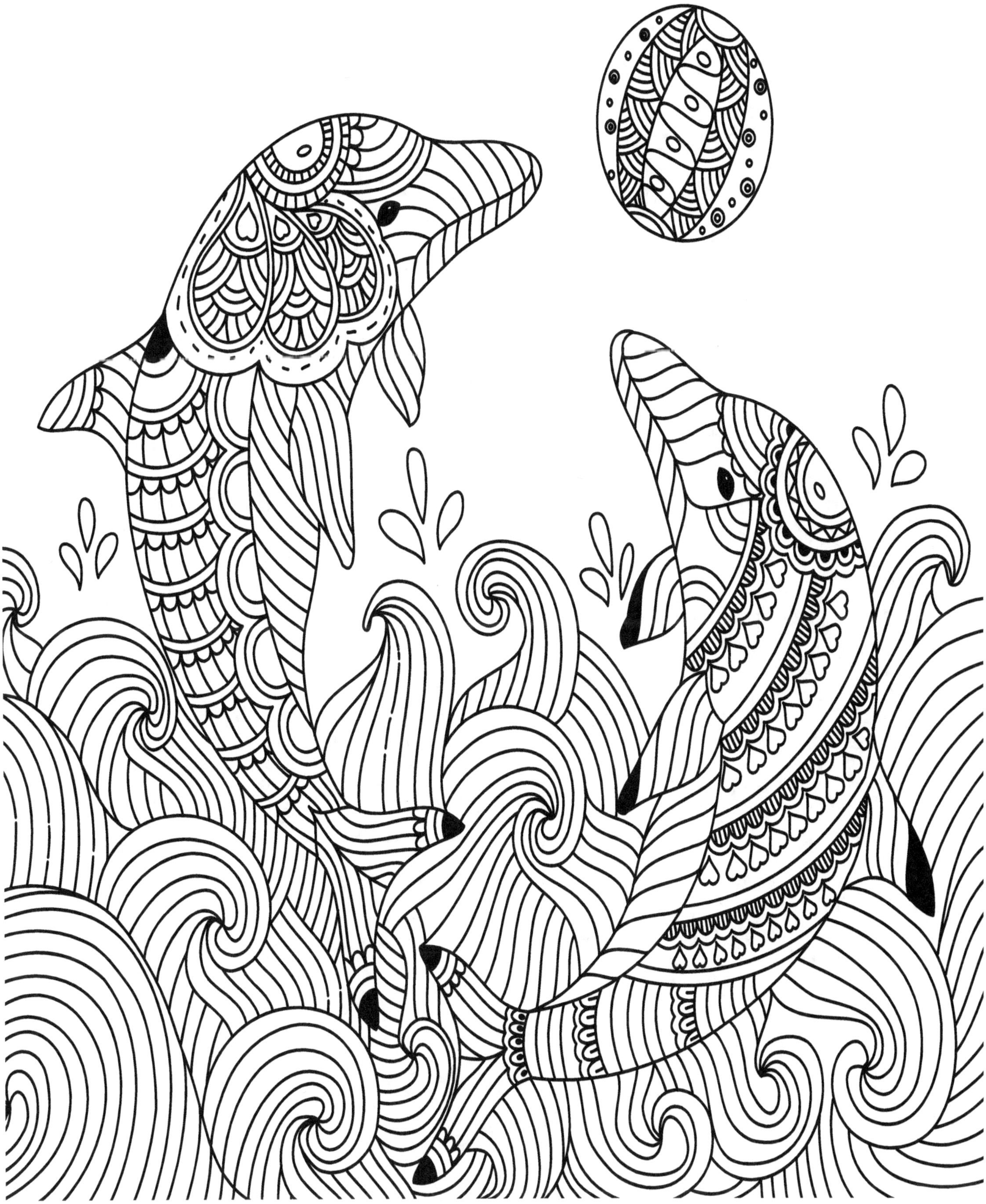

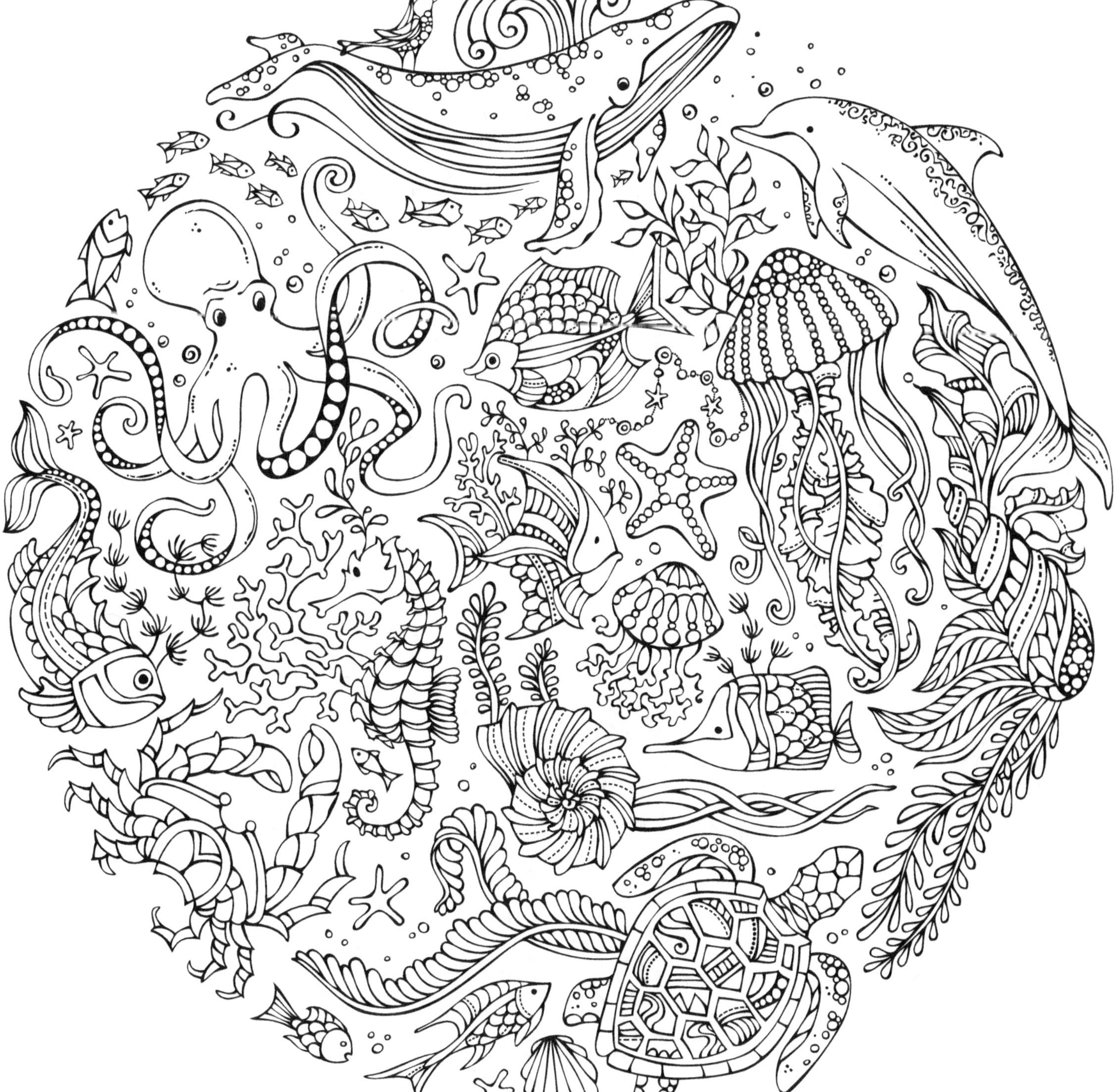

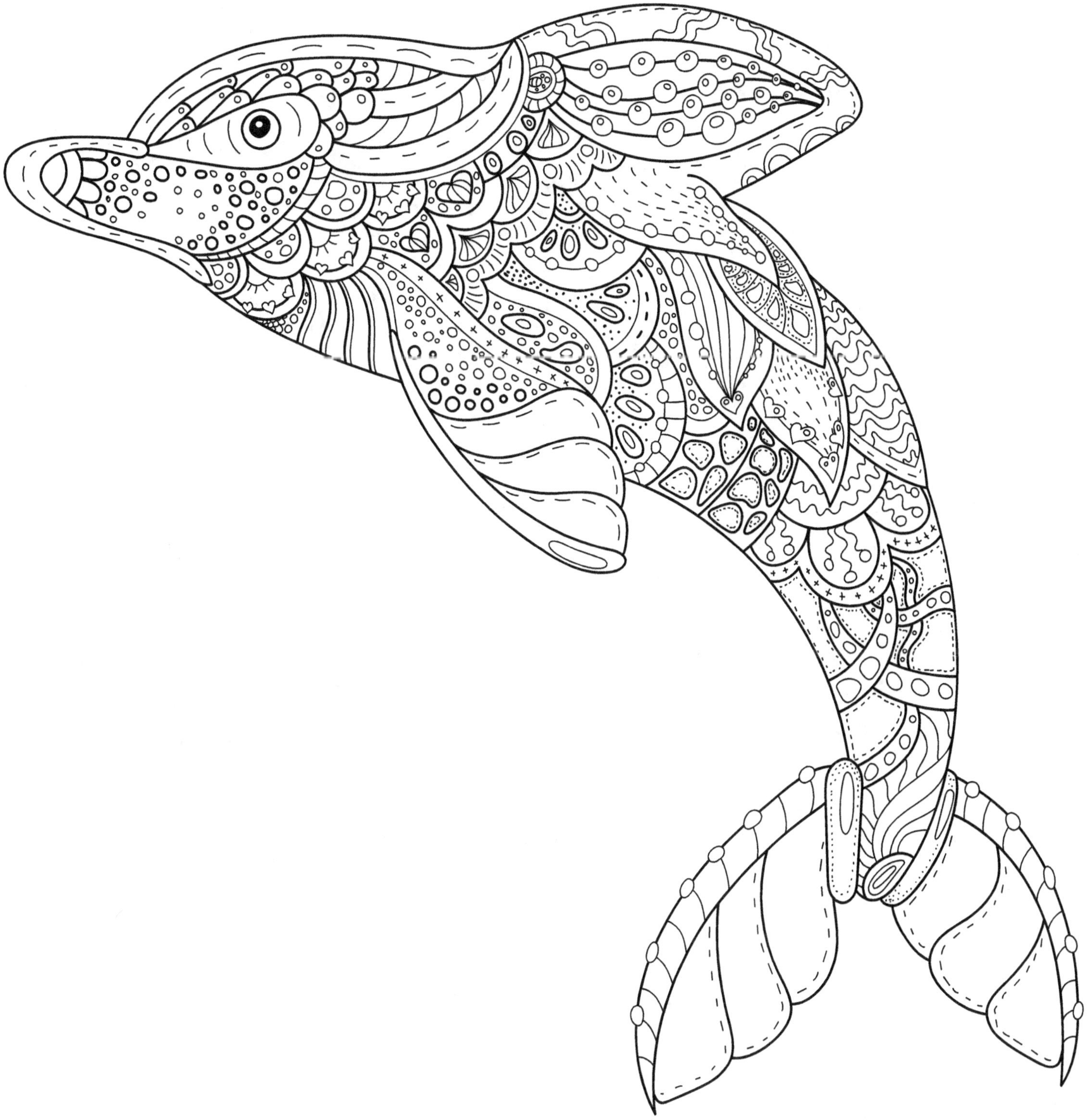

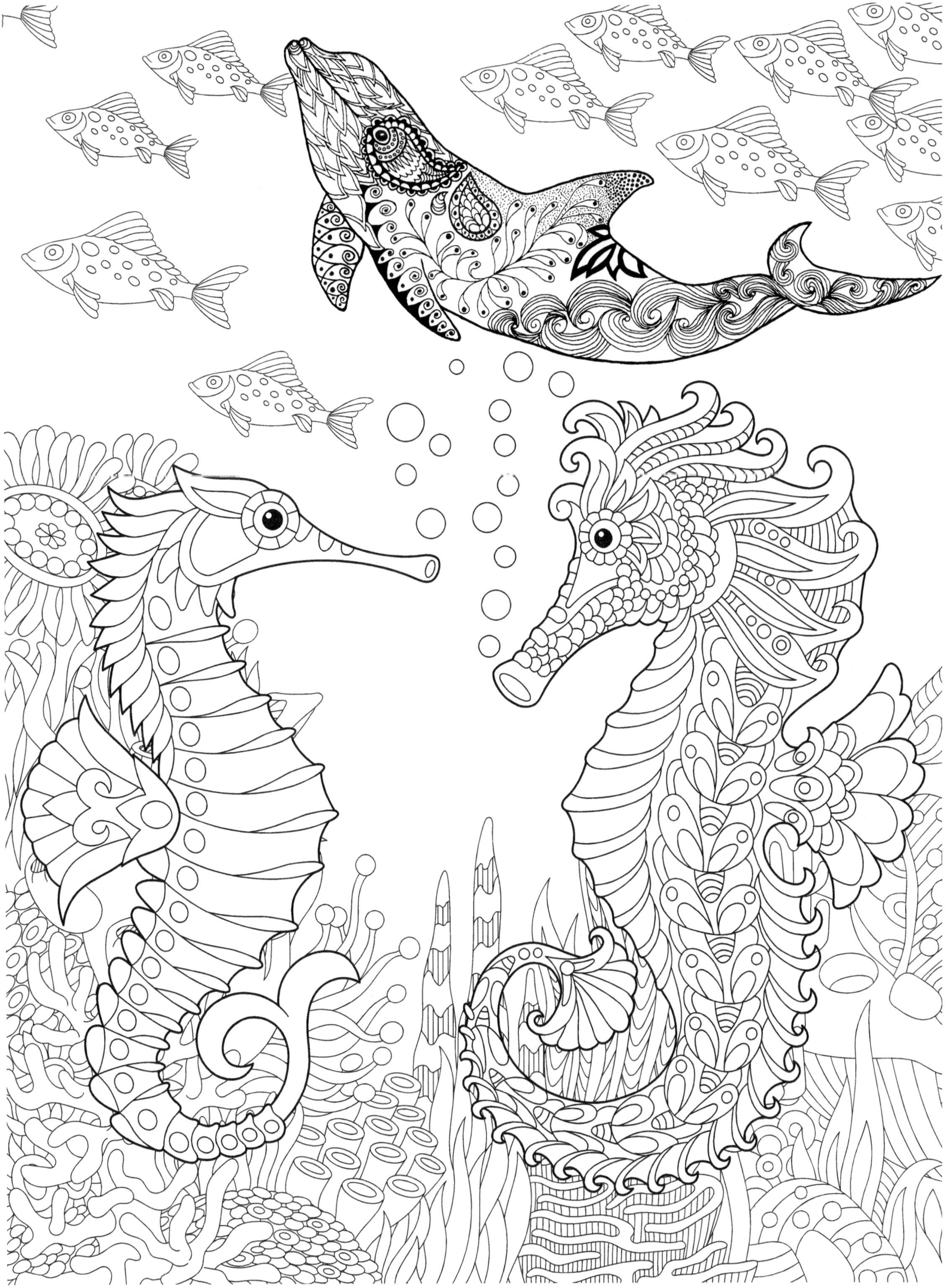

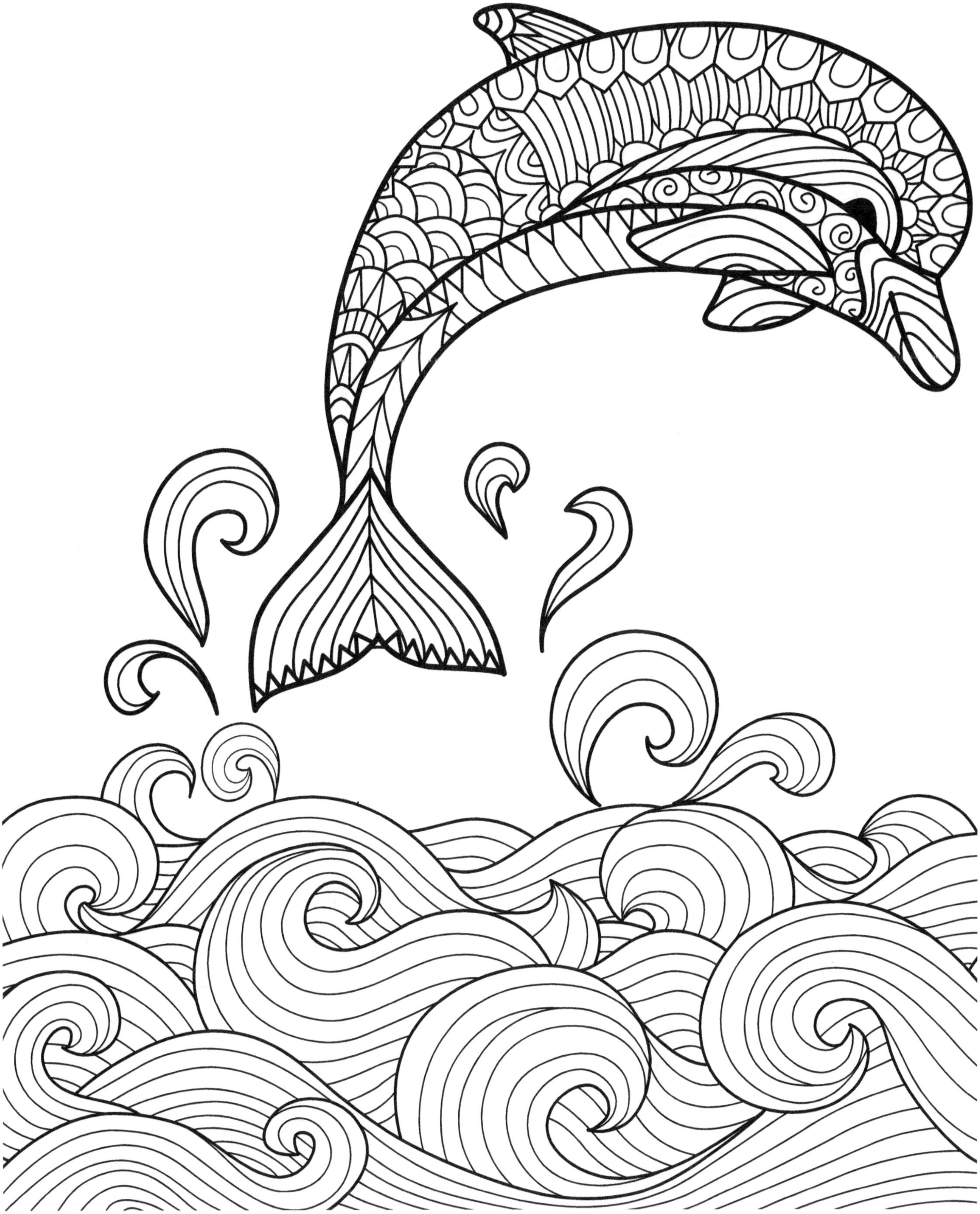

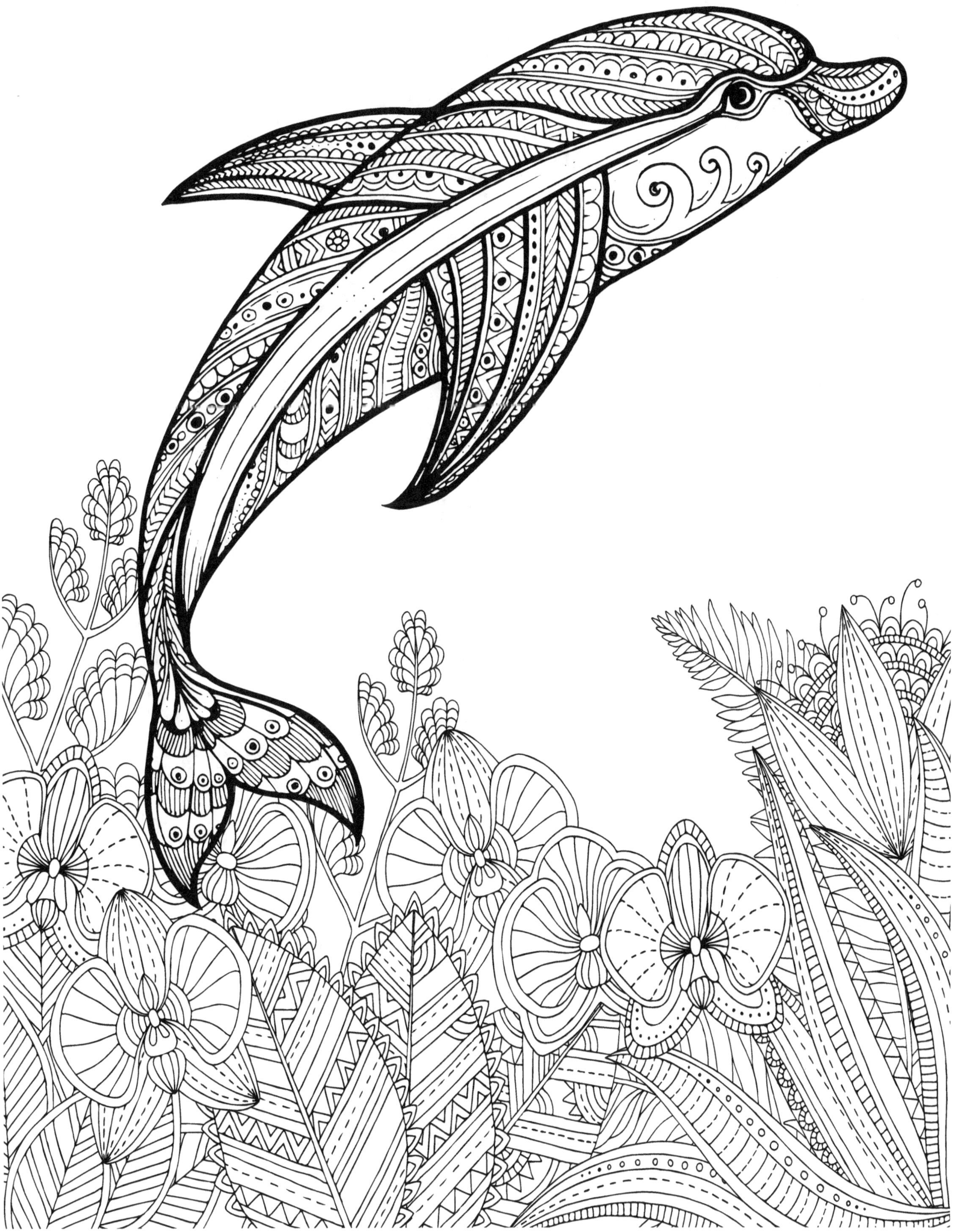

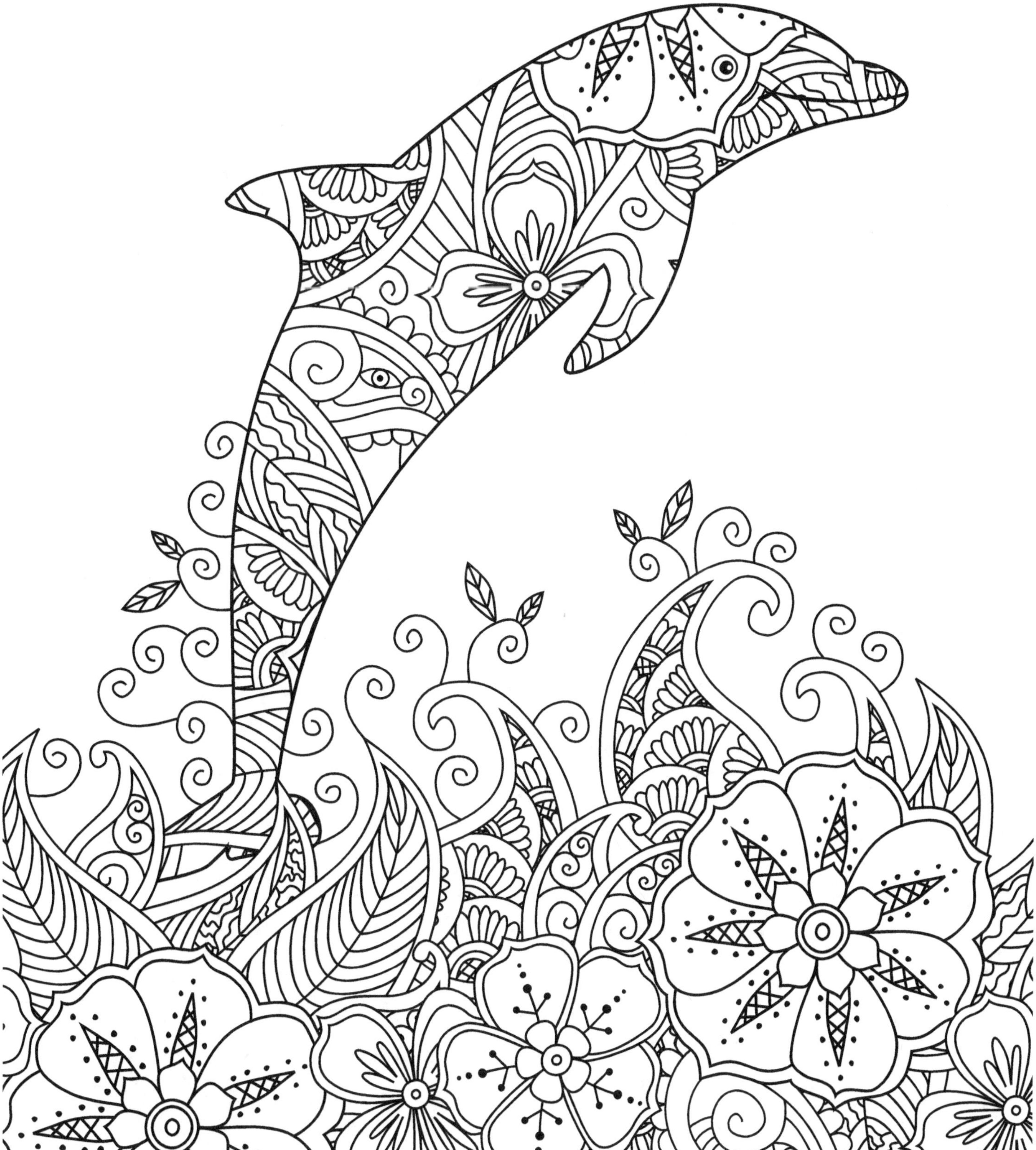

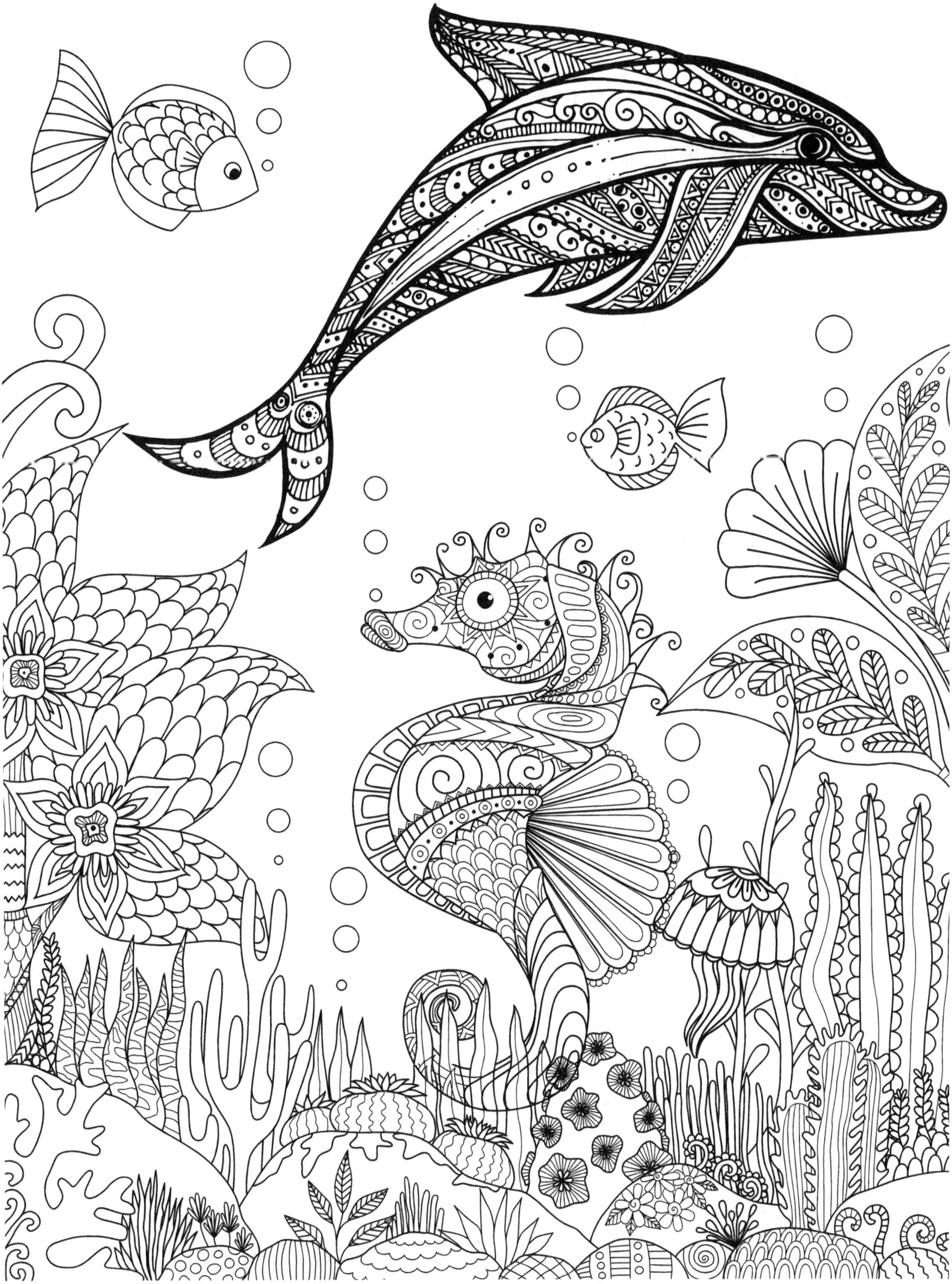

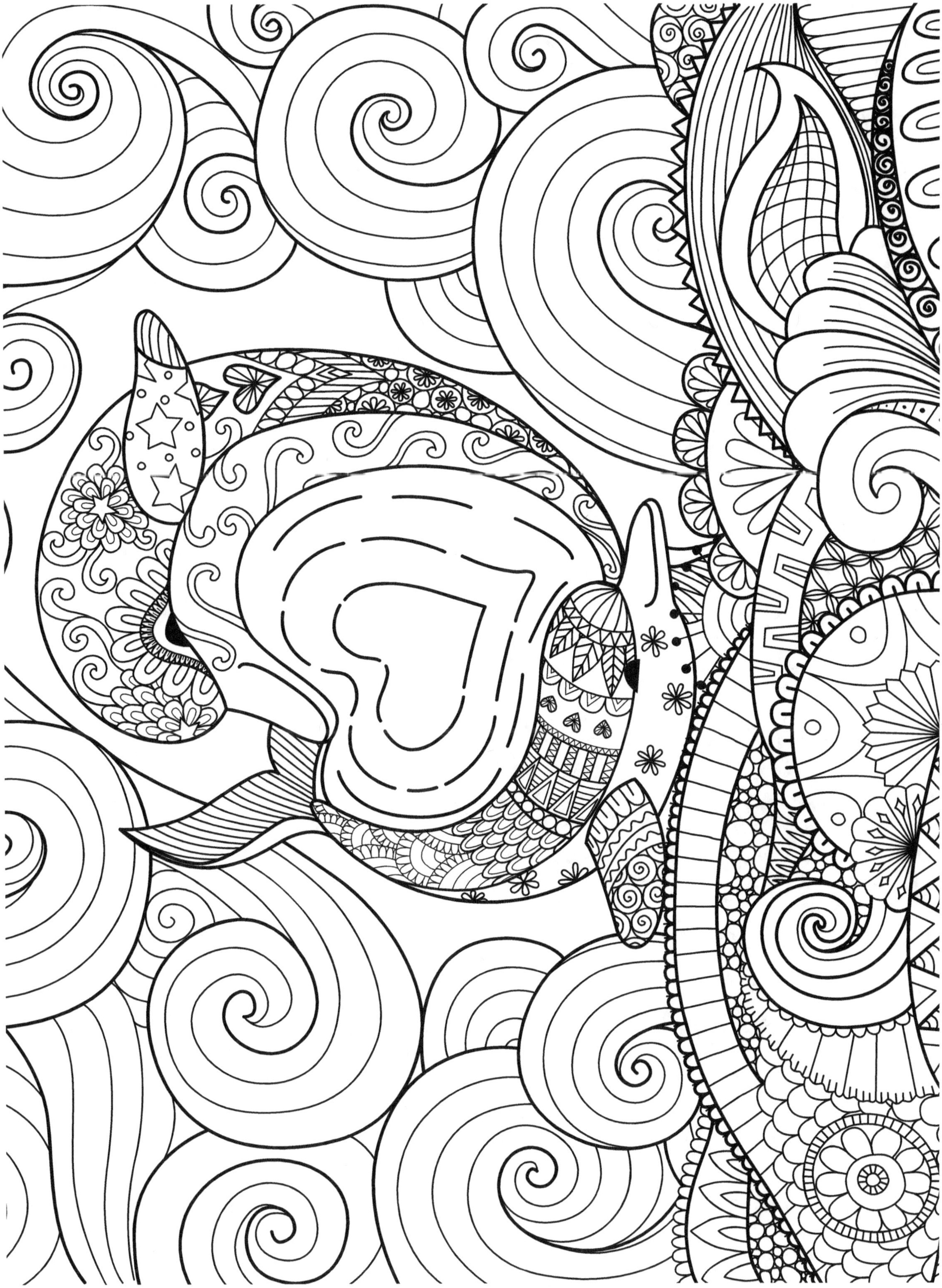

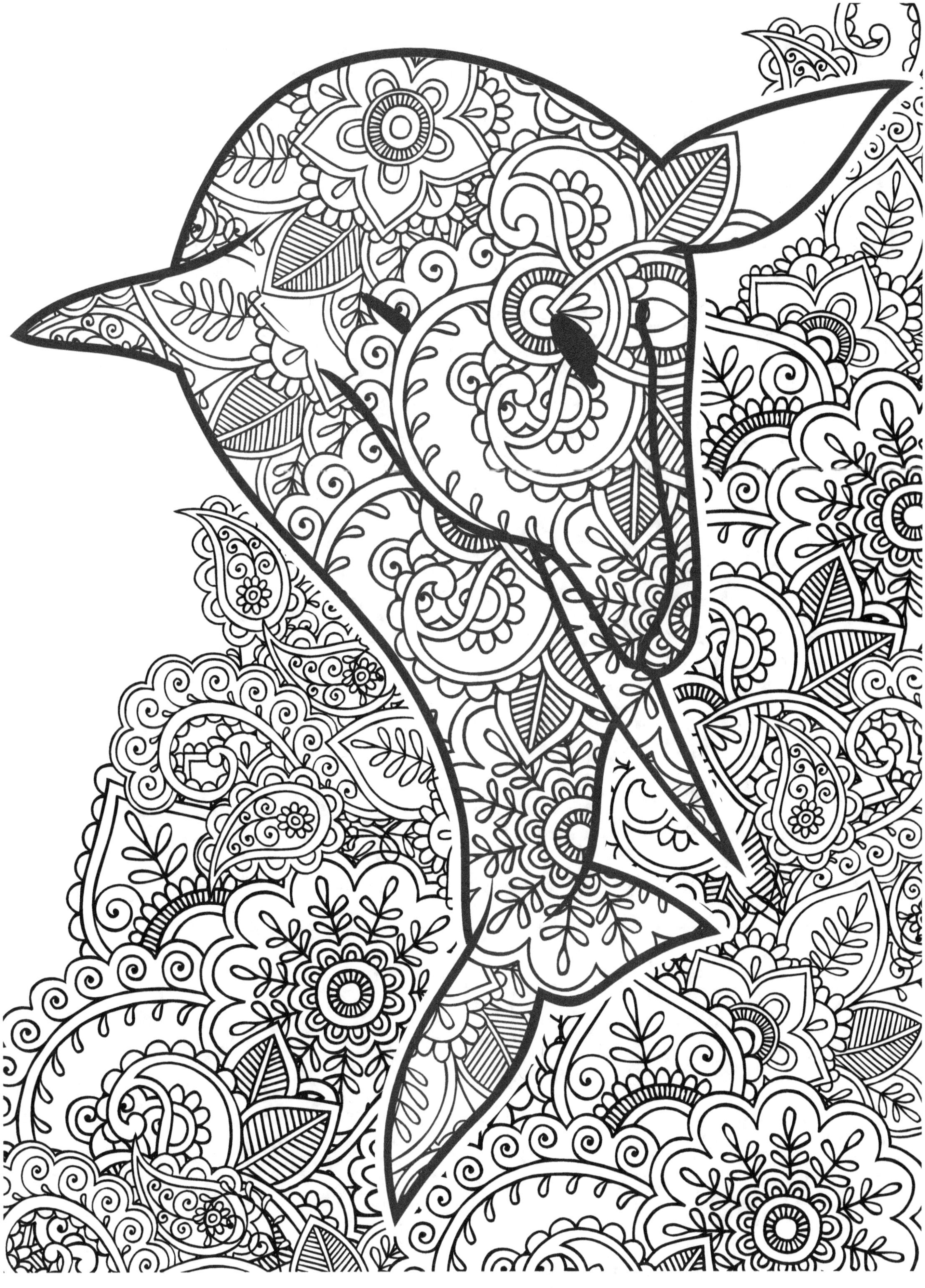

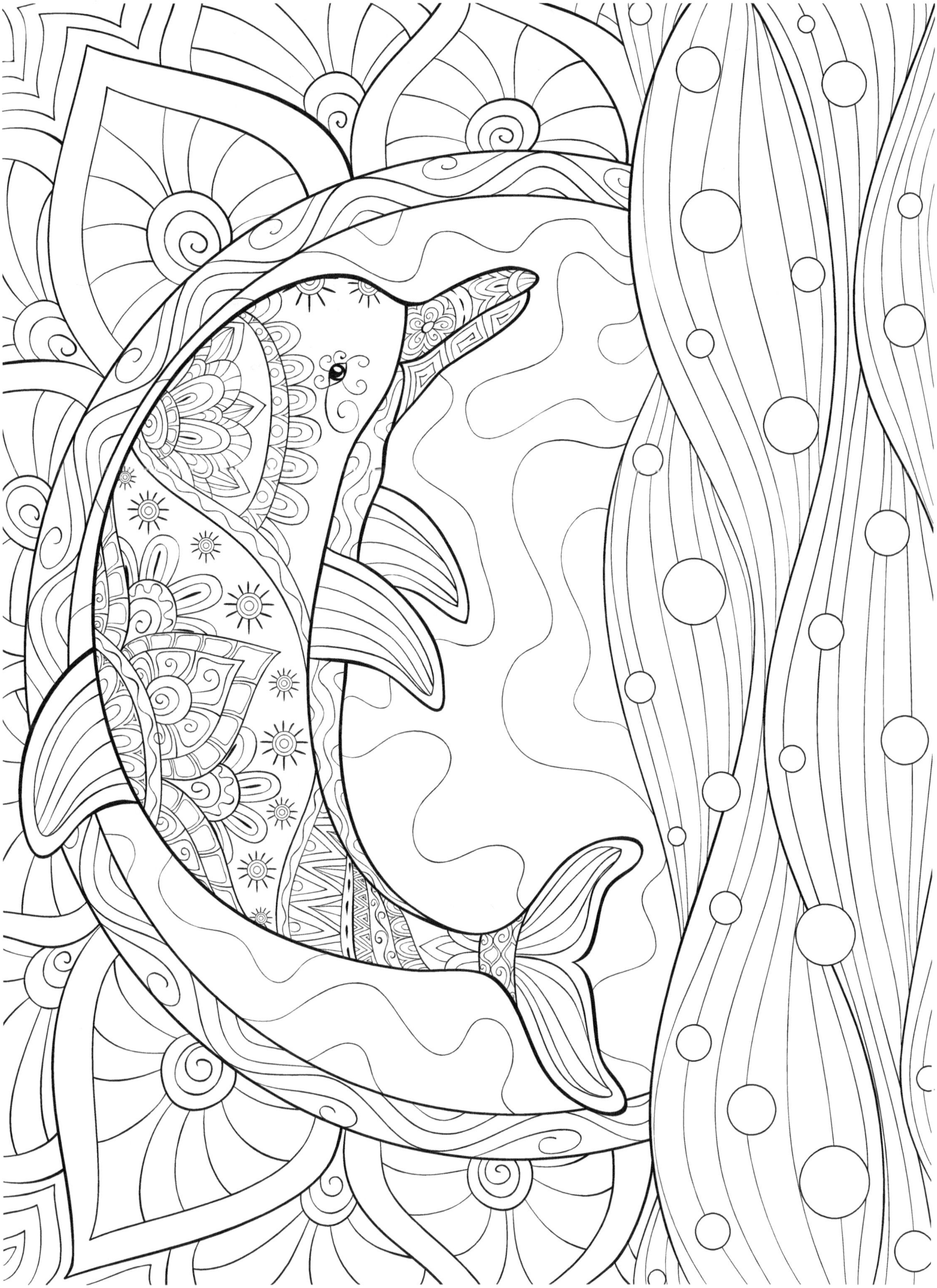

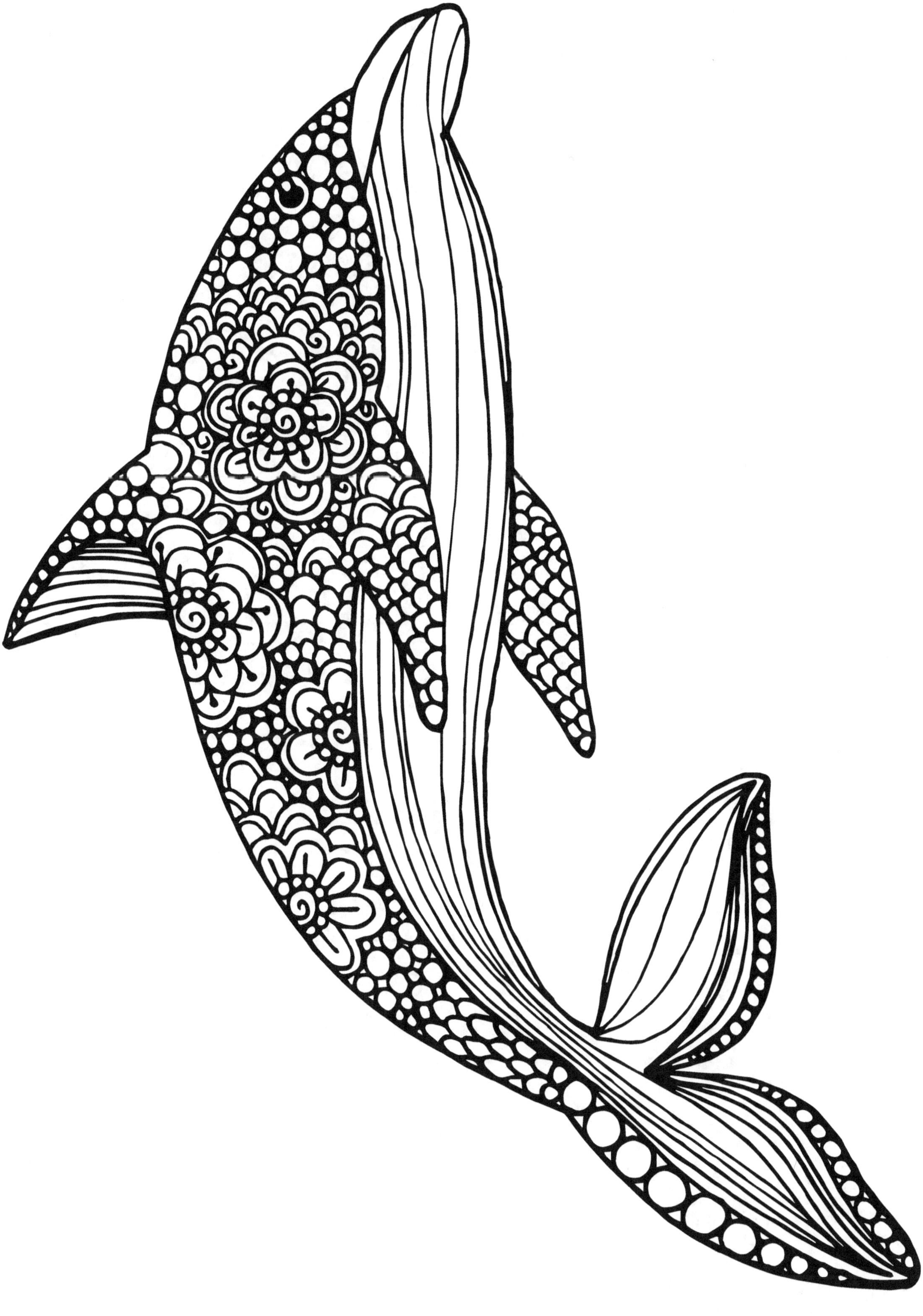

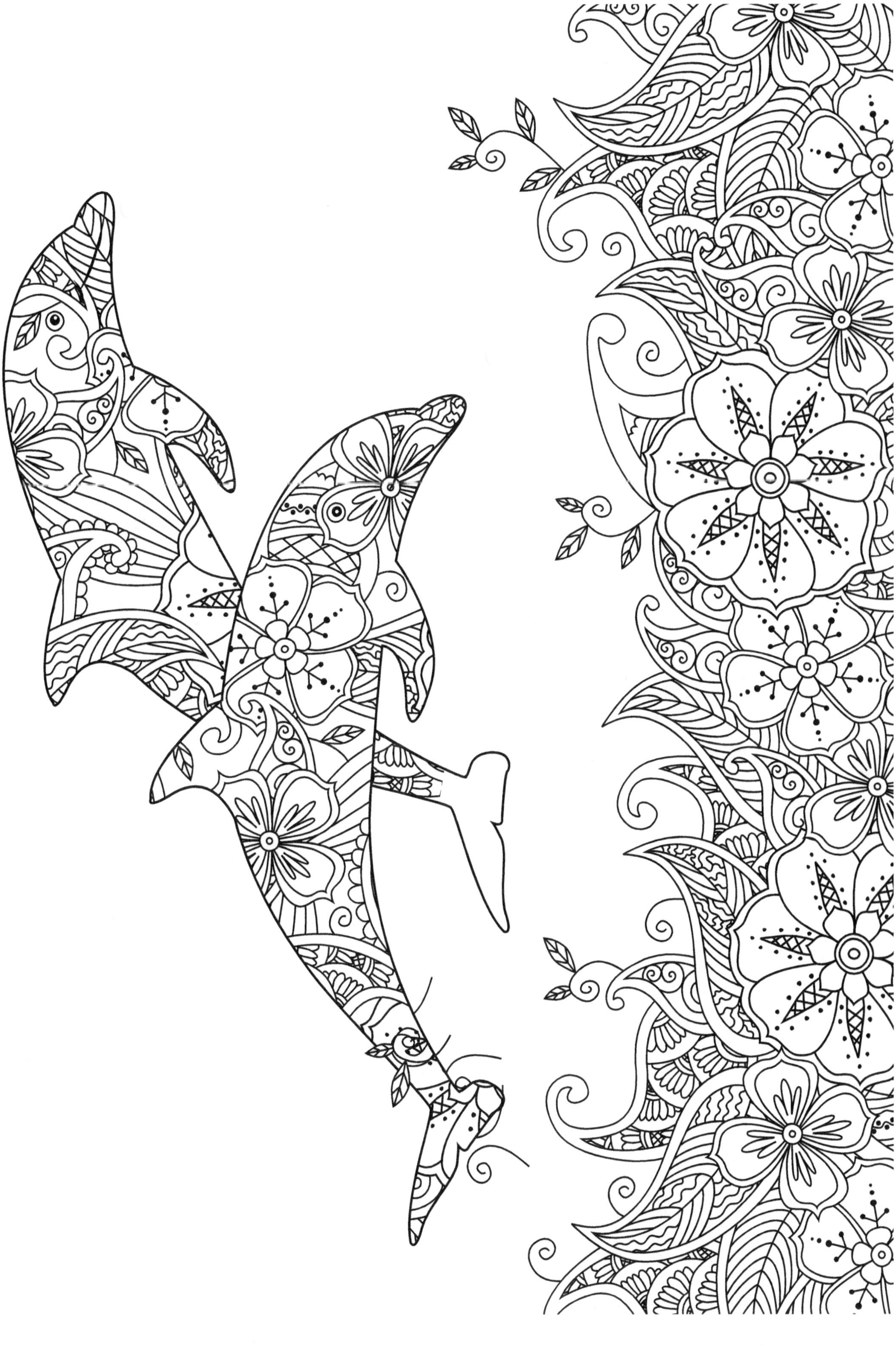

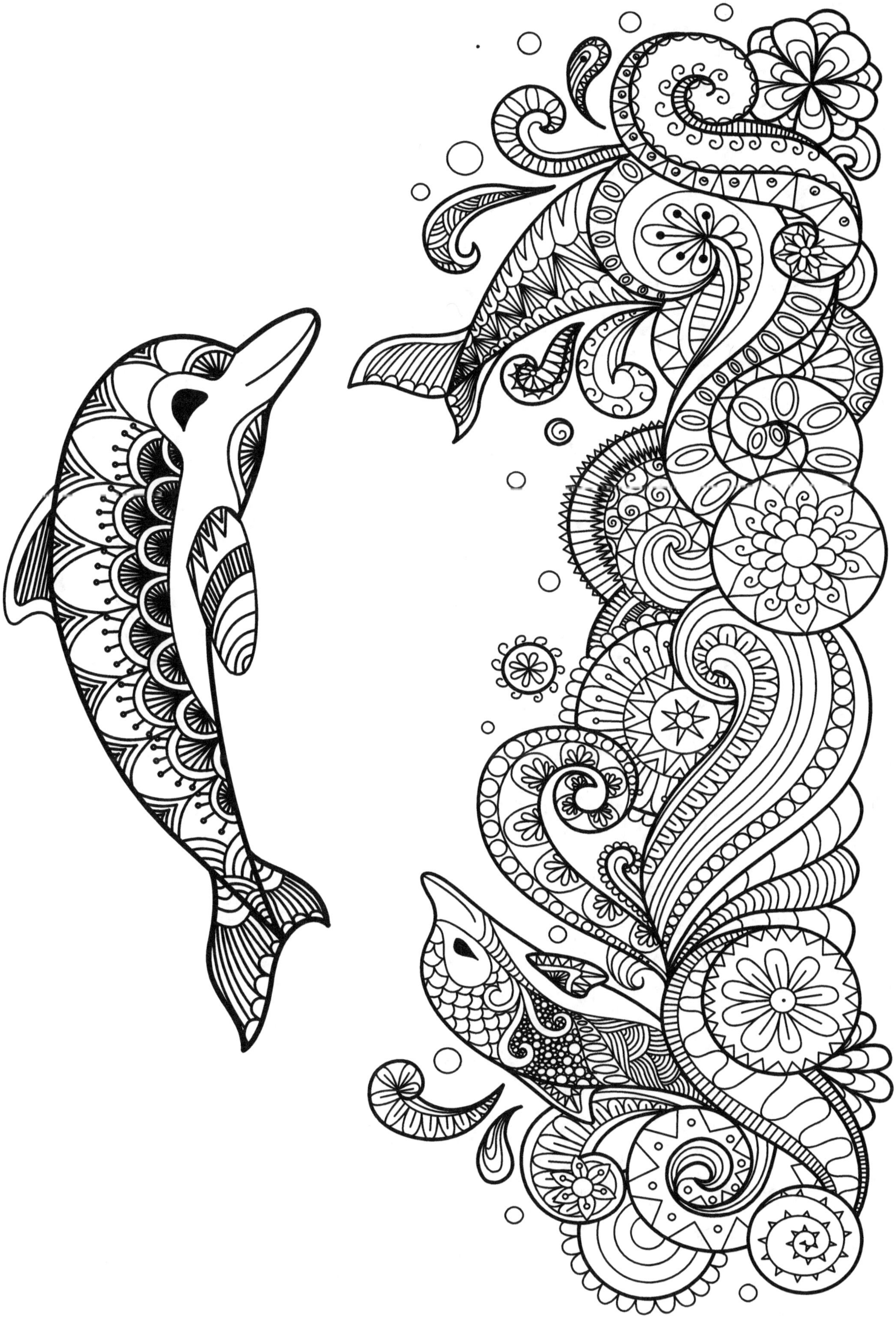

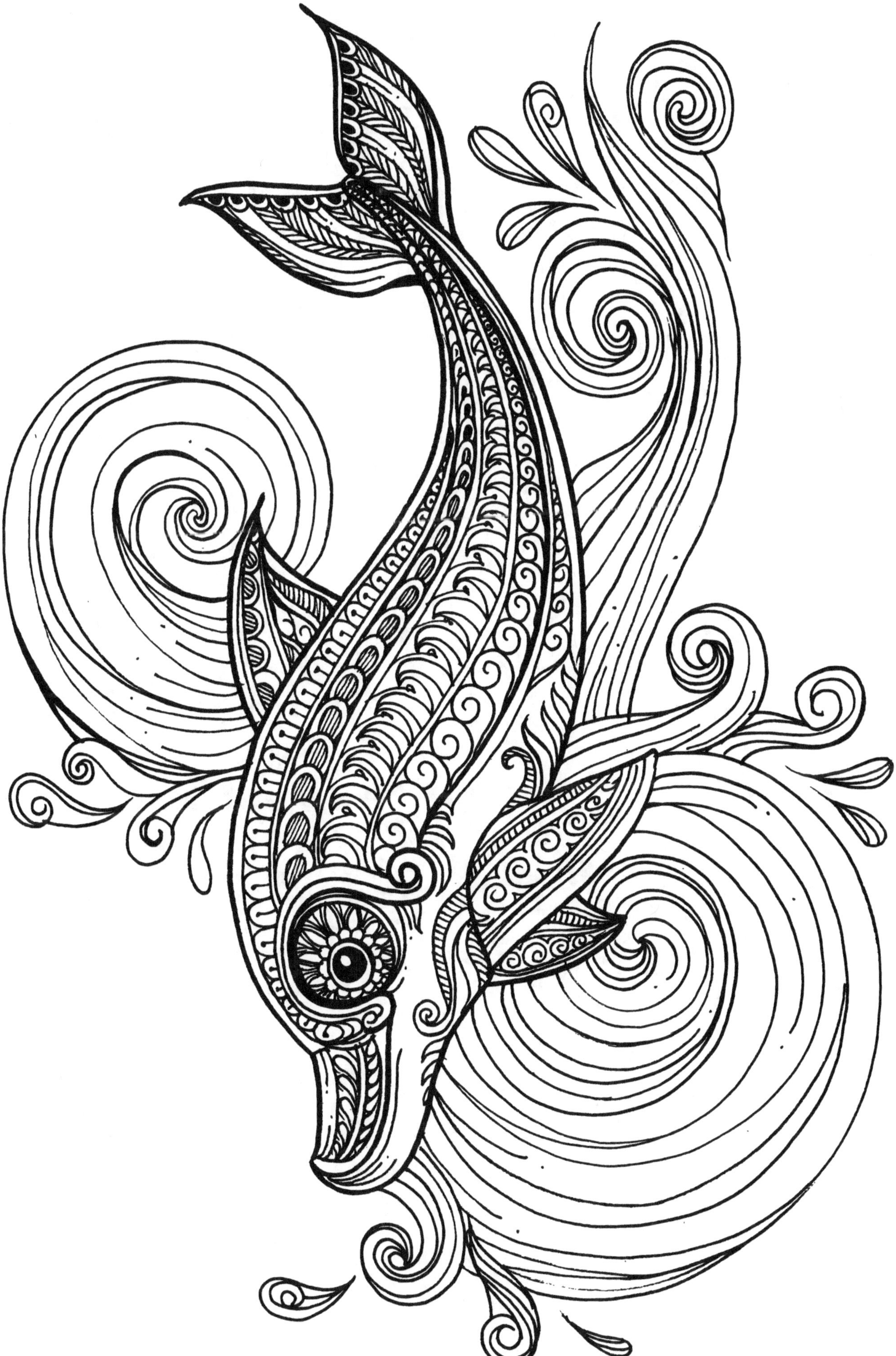

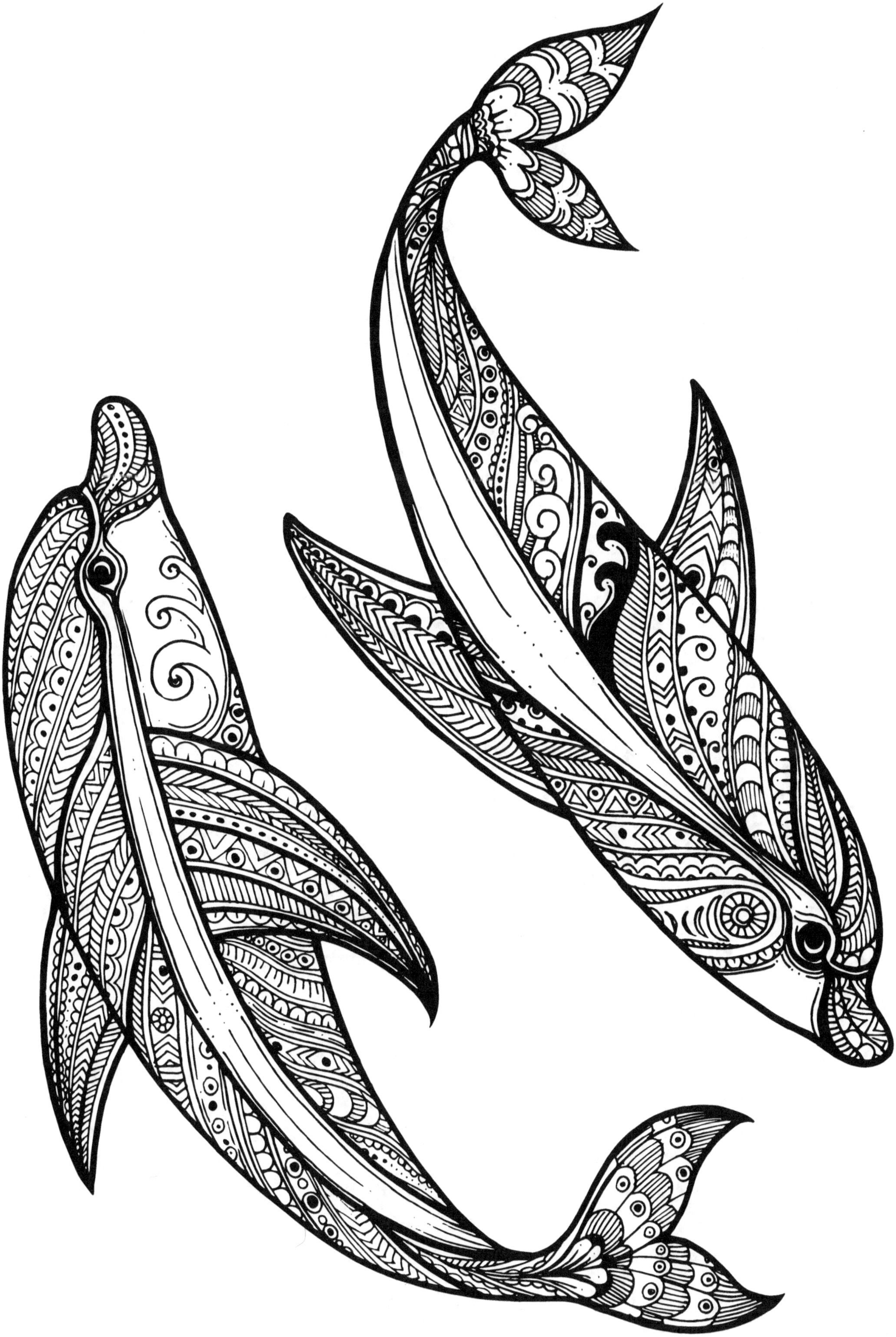

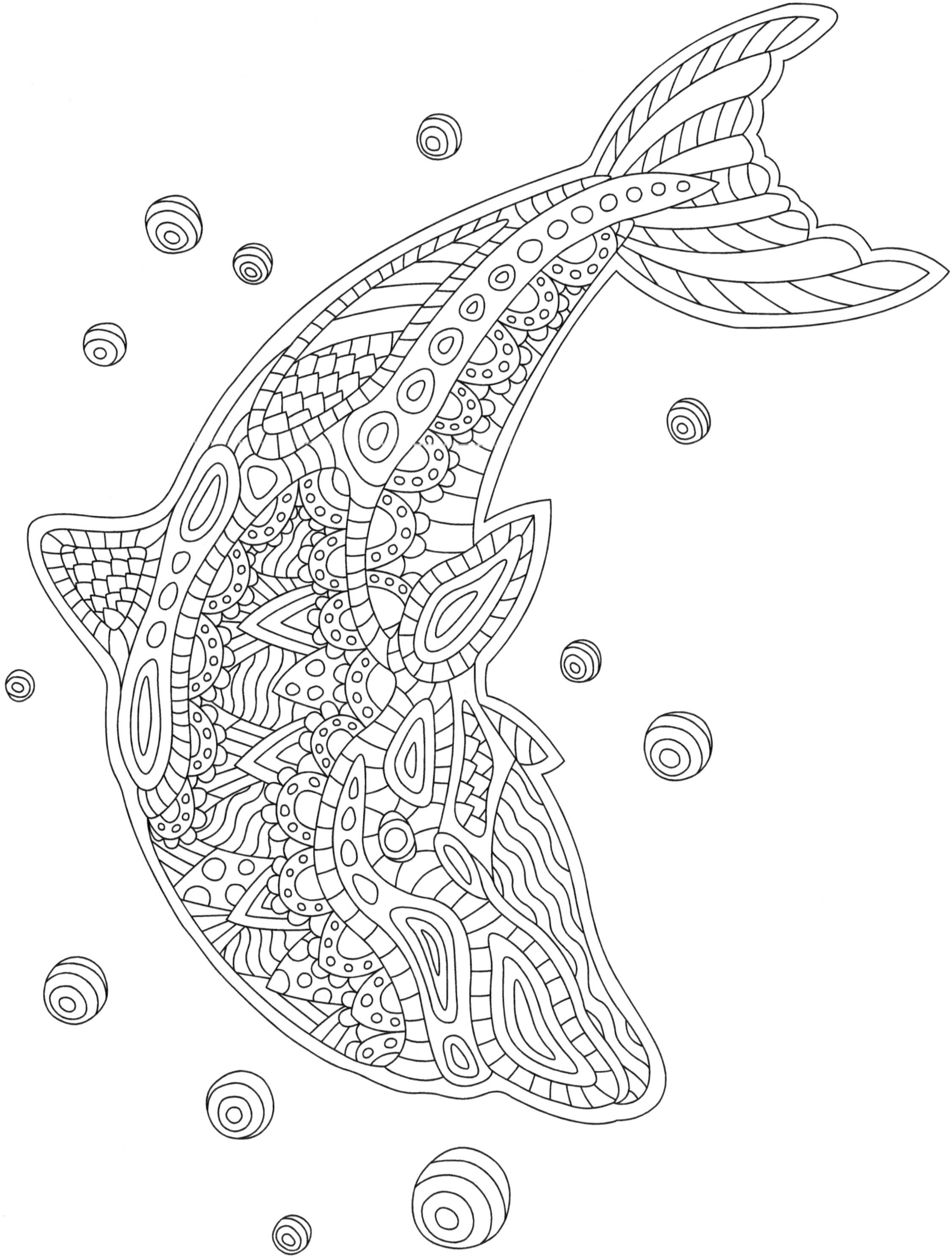

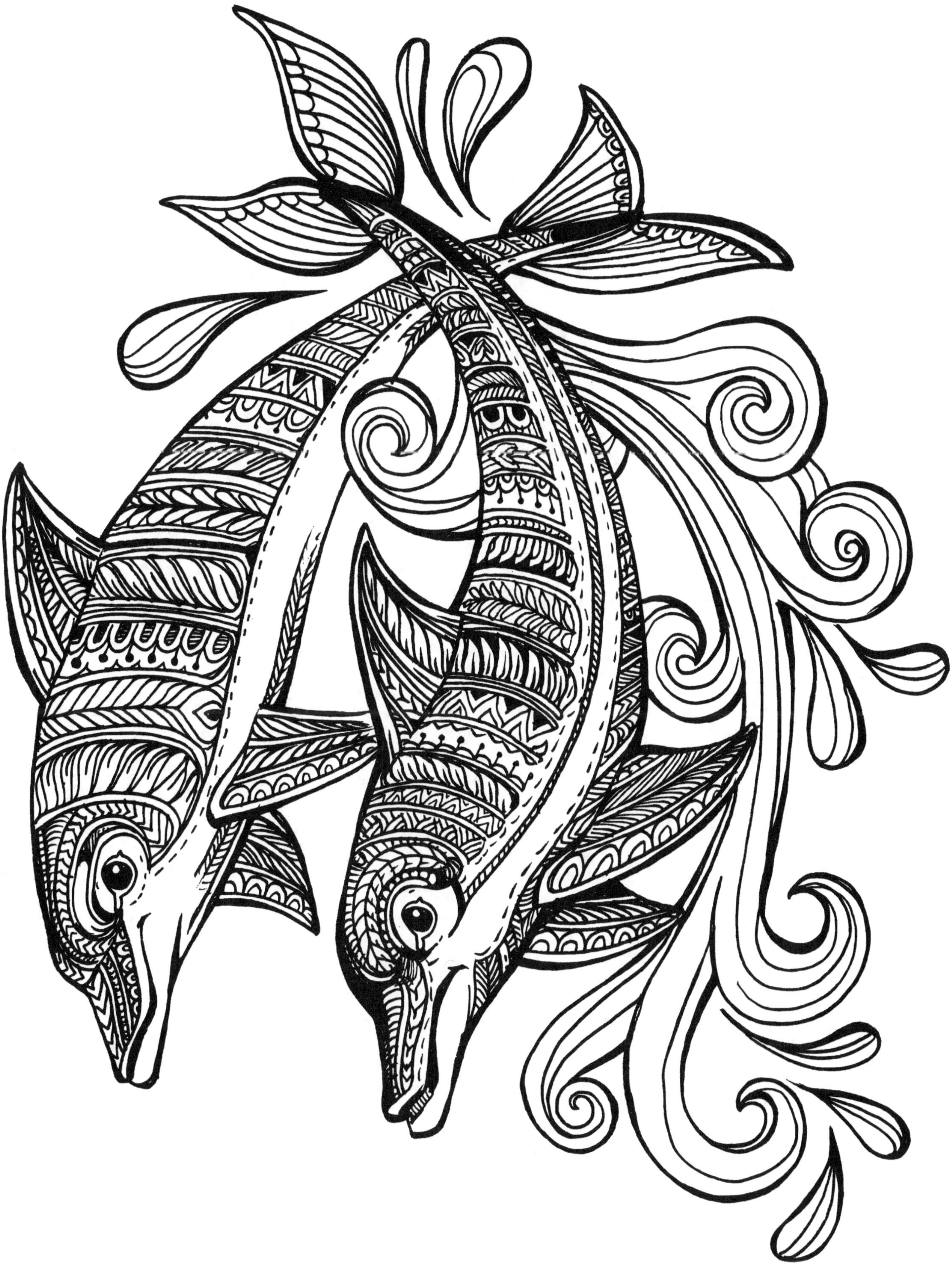

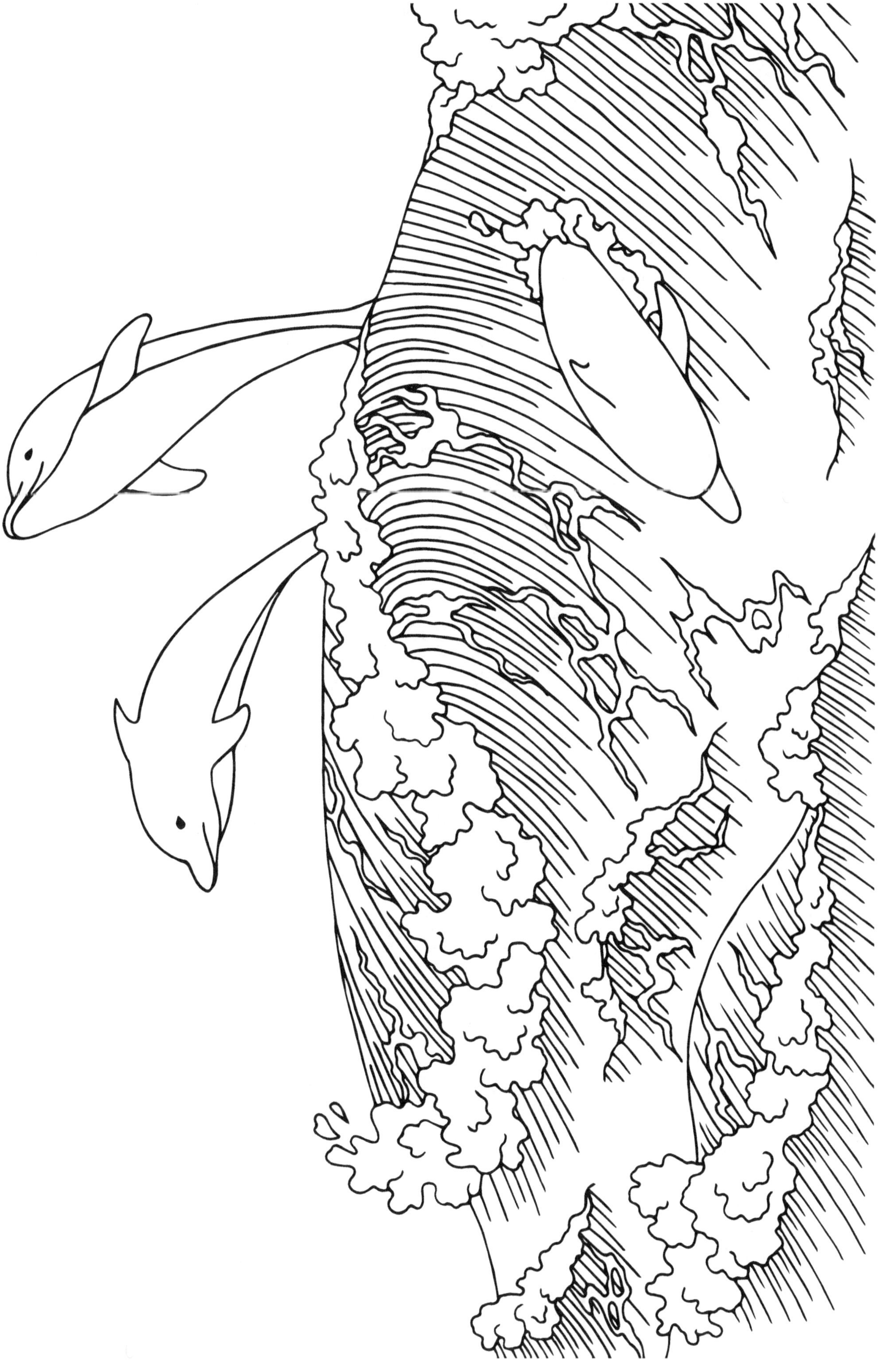

www.ingramcontent.com/pod-product-compliance
Lightning Source LLC
Chambersburg PA
CBHW062335220526
45469CB00008B/2721